Praise for
Messages Straight from the Heart:
Stories of Inspiration from Nevada

"A collaboration of 100 authors from all walks of life with the same message: Inspiration!"

— Nani Gomez, Author

"The perfect message for any challenge you are going through in your life!"

— Pat Hastings, Author of *Simply A Woman of Faith*

"Easy reading and the perfect message for each day."

— Juli Womack, Author

"Everyone has a story. Thank you to the 100 authors for sharing their story!"

— Jorge Colon, Author

"Finally a book with a positive message!"

— Joe Lopez, Author

"Perfect messages about how to achieve happiness in your life."

— Estaryia Venus

"A must read for anyone needing inspiration in their life!"

— Brian "Nugget" Boltood,
Author of *Promoting Positive*

"Timely book the world needs to hear to inspire people!"

—Julia Keiko Matsui Estrella, Author

INSIGHTFUL WORDS FOR EVERYDAY LIVING

MESSAGES
STRAIGHT FROM THE
HEART

STORIES OF INSPIRATION FROM NEVADA

LORI CHAFFIN

AVIVA
PUBLISHING
New York

**Messages Straight From The Heart:
Stories of Inspiration from Nevada**

Copyright © 2014 by Lori Chaffin

Published by:
Aviva Publishing
Lake Placid, NY
(518) 523-1320
www.AvivaPubs.com

Lori Chaffin
Email: MessagesFromTheHeart@yahoo.com

www.MessagesStrightFromTheHeart.com
www.HawaiiWellnessMagazine.com
www.HawaiiWellnessExpo.com

ISBN: 978-1-940984-61-2

Editor: Jody Rose
Cover Design: Angel Dog Productions / Nicole Gabriel
Interior Book Design: Angel Dog Productions / Nicole Gabriel

Every attempt has been made to source properly all quotes.

Printed in the United States of America

First Edition

2 4 6 8 10 12

♥

MESSAGES STRAIGHT FROM THE HEART

When I began my career in 1991 right after graduating from college, I was eager to soak up as much information as I could to advance my career as quickly as possible so that I could get on the fast track to achieving success.

As life unfolded in the years to come, I began to realize that there is more to life than career success. Whatever this 'more to life' is, or was, could be found in learning from the mistakes of others and their experiences, and overcoming obstacles by others ahead of me on this journey of life. And certainly by meeting with these people and speaking to them, they can share with us their traveled the path on their journey for our benefit.

What I discovered was that in order to avoid the same mistakes that others made the best way to do this was to both read the stories of others and interview others who had traveled the road ahead. As a result, I became obsessed with reading biographies, interviewing my elders and studying both the successes and failures of others in an attempt to apply these lessons to my life.

What I have learned is that successful people emulate the actions of other successful people while avoiding the actions (or inaction) of other people who have failed. As a result, this line of thinking allows you to super accelerate your journey and allows you to attract more success into your life, avoid failure, while throughout the process taking time out to live in the now, enjoy the journey, be happy and appreciate all the blessings that we have in our lives.

In this powerful book compiled by Lori Chaffin (and 100 other contributing authors), you will learn all the strategies, techniques and ideas needed to live a 'heart-centered' life that will allow you to achieve serenity, happiness and prosperity (both financially and emotionally). As a result of applying the many years of wisdom in this book by these contributing authors, you will achieve this bliss far sooner they you would if making your journey alone.

In *Messages Straight from the Heart*, you will hear first-hand from 100 of Nevada's most talented writers, thinkers, philosophers, coaches and thought leaders of our day. This book is truly the 'best of the best, and the combined wisdom in this book is like having a complete library of our 100 plus books at your side, all neatly organized in one resource to assist you in your journey to peace, love and tranquility!

When you apply the wisdom, poems, quotes, and real life experiences of these thought leaders to your life, you will be able to achieve career success, deep and meaningful relationships, and steer clear from the many pitfalls and obstacles that life may try and throw at you. These messages from the hearts of Nevada's best authors will propel your life to a higher level and you will achieve success in all areas of your life much quicker than had you not been blessed with this gift!

You will learn how to achieve the specific knowledge that eludes most people in this world. You will learn the secret to achieving happiness, joy and learn the power of living in the moment, stepping into your becoming and unleashing your passions to propel you to live a life straight from your heart that you have always aspired to live.

Throughout this book you will learn that you are the driving force to your life, you pick your destiny based on "choice" not by "chance." You become the unstoppable force of power to live your life by intention, serve others, and achieve your life goals as a result.

Most importantly you will learn how to harness the power of a "heart-centered" life to find your bliss, serve others and achieve a life of meaningful purpose as a result.

You will be inspired to forgive, let go of your past, set the reset button of your life, and begin each new day with joy in your heart and determination in your soul make a better life for you and your loved ones!

So get ready for any exciting journey! Get ready to meet

Nevada's best and brightest, and most talented writers and thought leaders of our time. Get ready for an exciting journey into your mind, your heart, and soul, to be equipped with the skills, mindset, and attitude needed for you to create your own destiny and live a heart-centered life!

To your success, from my heart to yours!

Patrick Snow

International Best-Selling Author of
Creating Your Own Destiny, The Affluent Entrepreneur, and *Boy Entrepreneur*

www.PatrickSnow.com
www.ThePublishingDoctor.com

ACKNOWLEDGMENTS

Messages Straight From The Heart: Stories of Inspiration from Nevada is an intimate collection of wishes, prayers and stories from authors who write to humanity from their homes in Nevada. This collection, compiled by Lori Chaffin, and includes heartfelt words from individuals from age 15+ with different backgrounds. This is a poignant, integrated body of work that expresses the simple sincerity of inspiration and the love so many across the world currently seek.

The authors in this publication were selected because of each one's ability to convey a personal wish to promote inspiration to the world. Some writers are being published for the first time, and others are experienced professionals. Some entries are entertaining and fun, and some are serious, but every voice is unique. This book series of collections empower human beings to write down positive stories in ways that inspire others. All of the submissions appear as close to the original forms as possible, with minimal changes.

I would like to recognize and thank the following for their messages and gifts to the world that appear in this book:

Darlene Mea, Adrianne Carlino Gentile,
Rev. Dr. Edwige Bingue, Dennis Krum, Tish Mezell,
Mitzi Reed, Danny Vegas, Jamie Lee, Charmaine Lee,
Tammy Shaw-Grabel, Susan M. Wright, Patricia Brown,
Catherine Ormand, Reverend Thabiti,
Carrie Leigh Sandoval,
Maureen Pua' ena O'Shaughnessy, Xena Foreman,
Lynn Boland, Danielle Dove, Nalani Malia Paliotta,
Navjit Kandola, Erin Pavlina, Victorya Campe,
Barbara Berg, Sarah Michaels, DeAnne Wolfgram,
DW Grant, Chip Evans, Annabelle Husson,
Anita Babinszki, Cathy Pagano, Vickie Wilson,
Vernon J Davis Jr., Heather Bruton, Emahmn,
Cielja Kieft, Jill Bachhuber, Morgan St. James,
Kathleen Berry, Steve Pavlina, Rebecca Fountain,
Jamillah Ali Rashada, Monica Johnson-Williams,
Imelda Perez McCarthy, Nicholas Marco,
Andres Fragoso, Jr., Regina Rose Murphy,
Rick Sorensen, Glen Alex, Boni Stewart, Deborah Berry,
Marquetta Goodwin, Char Modelle, Sharon Chayra,
Jan Hogan, Jon Carl Olson, Donna Thomas,
Cynthia Walker, Dan Klatt, Vernon J Davis Jr.,
Eric J Tischler, Anette Lachowski, Lila Penn,
Tamia Dow, Janet Dunnagan, Janelle Ross,
Dr. AlixSandra Parness, John Tyler, Mary Chambers,
Jacie Urquidi-Maynard.

Thank you to our Corporate Sponsors.

702 Events for your website that connects everyone in Las Vegas. www.702events.com

Publishing Coach, Patrick Snow for his support and guidance throughout this project. And his continued assistance to the many authors and people all over the world who have a story that they wish to share by publishing a book. For a complimentary publishing consultation visit:

www.ThePublishingDoctor.com

CONTENTS

♥

HOLD YOUR FORK,
THE BEST IS YET TO COME!

After you have finished a meal and the waiter is taking your empty plates, they will tell you "Hold Your Fork, The Best Is Yet To Come!" Meaning the dessert is on the way and keep your fork so you can enjoy what's coming. The best part of the meal is about to arrive!

I am sure a lot of people have gone through challenges, learning lessons and changes in Nevada and around the world in the past few years. We have all grown and taken these learning lessons into 2014 and beyond. With every new adventure, I keep hearing in my head the waiter telling me to hold my fork, the best is yet to come.

I take all my new friendships, experiences, ideas and inspiration from my past with excitement into my future.
I am sitting holding my fork waiting for the waiter to bring me the best part of the meal, along with everyone around me that has challenged, inspired, pushed, pulled, screamed, and cheered for me along the way.

This is my story, and here are their stories…

Looking forward to seeing you healthy, happy and inspired in 2014 and beyond!

Love & Light,

Lori Chaffin

Lori Chaffin, Las Vegas & Hawaii
Author of Messages Straight From The Heart Series
Publisher of Hawaii Wellness Directory
www.MessagesStraightFromTheHeart.com
www.HawaiiWellnessMagazine.com

♥

ZEN CITY VEGAS, WHERE LIFE IS ZEN-FULL ALL THE TIME...

I'm not sure how I ended up in Las Vegas, why I'm still here or why I keep coming back. I hear this story over and over from amazing beings now living and loving Las Vegas – the unknown vortex, in the desert!

I remember clearly, arriving in Las Vegas on vacation... my very first thought was, "do people actually live here and how could they?" It looked like glitter gulch, bright lights, brick and mortar, seemingly *devoid of LIFE, as we know it.* It appeared to be SIN city for sure and *NO place for nature or natural girl* like myself... What am I thinking to even consider living here? And so, for my 'sister' I would live in this mirage in the desert, only for 1 year... That was 33 years ago and the 250 thousand beings in 1979, became 2 million in 2014! What an incredible journey it has been... I have learned so much!

What I learned very quickly is; *to live & thrive in chaos, we must stay in balance.* It was something I just knew deeply, so I began my exploration into new dimensions of

Las Vegas that did not seem apparent, on the surface. I've since discovered more than I could have ever imagined. I found dimensions of life, reality and my relationship to living in this reality to be filled with diversity, choices, imagination, timeless time, amazing beings, no boundaries and the importance of doing 'the work' to stay in balance.

Not sure about you, however, *nature is my sanctuary*. Las Vegas is surrounded by mountains. The valley is geographically bounded by the Spring Mountains and Red Rock Canyon to the west, Frenchman Mountain and Lake Mead to the east, the McCullough Range to the south, and the Sheep and Las Vegas ranges to the north. With this I have lived in heaven on earth –a timeless city where there are no rules, (pretty much) in a location surrounded by nature. AND, here's a secret, only a small percentage of the 2 million residents get out into nature – so it's even that more enjoyable!

What has been the most surprising thing to me is the level of awakened beings that make Las Vegas their home, or home away from home. I see it like this. In life yen and yang exist; it's the balance of all things, visible and invisible. In Las Vegas the 'light beings' are extra bright to create the balance, therefore the 'light beings' are truly amazing, yet pretty much incognito. As I mentioned earlier, 'the rules are different here, on many levels, therefore 'light beings here don't look like GURUS, they look like, suits, dancers, union workers, card dealers, homeless, CEOs and me!' – *We're all the same, yet all very UniqUe…*

AND, I believe this to be the same all over the world; we are all the same, yet very different…We can thank LIFE for this, because conscious creation moves through us, as us, in all things, in infinite expressions.

As the publisher/editor of New Dimensions Magazine in the late 80's early 90's, what seemed 'le Natural to life' for me, was apparently way ahead of its time… Now in 2014, I see Vegas as ZEN City Vegas, TM, a city where we can be in balance all the time if we know where to go and what to do AND are open to multi-dimensional realities and beings… Of course it's not easy living in the land of pure unadulterated possibilities and temptations of every kind… I say, *such is life, find your balance, your Zenfull side and, IN JOY the journey…*

Darlene Mea, Las Vegas
www.facebook.com/ZENCityVegas
Author of *Lose Your Mind Gain Your Sanity*

♥

ENJOYING LIFE IN LAS VEGAS

A yearning stirs in my soul within
A passion, no breath could fill.
Only a miracle of nature, I know
Will replenish my spiritual thrill.
I go to Red Rock Canyon to ride a horse,
Take a dip in snow-melted streams,
Hike up cliffs, repel myself down,
Walk in the Ancient Ones
dreams,
Then eavesdrop on birds, watch butterflies dance
And sniff sweet desert perfumes.
I feel refreshed, my soul reborn;
My spirit once again blooms.
A calling awakens within my brain
This could be my lucky day.
I gather the charms important to me,
Look for clues as I wend my way.
I implore her, "Please, be good to me!"
And I feed her my silver and gold.
At first, she does not seem to respond.
Then I win all that my pockets can hold.
Excitement starts thumping a beat in my heart.
I need creative inspirations,
Galleries, museums, Broadway shows,

And the Art District presentations.
I swim with the dolphins, and then go to a spa,
Listen to jazz musicians play,
Disappear into magic, dance at a nightclub,
And soar high with a Cirque du Soleil.
The Ballet, Philharmonic, so much talent to see.
It is difficult choosing just one.
Hilarious comedians, shows for free.
Each day can be filled with such fun.
A rumble starts growing from deep inside
Nourishment is what I crave
Exotic cuisine from top chefs in the world
are available in every enclave.
Then it's on to another goodwill event
In Vegas we do more than, ease strife.
We give of ourselves, our time, and our gifts
To make sure all here share a good life.
I take a ride when I've had my fill
Up a mountain or down to the lake
Watch the stars or a maybe a meteor shower
And think of a poem that my thoughts can make.
I am so lucky to live in Las Vegas
And satisfy body, spirit, and mind,
For this is just what I did today.
I wonder tomorrow, what will I find?

Adrianne Carlino Gentile, Las Vegas
Author of *66 LEAVES Poems from My Tree of Life*

♥

THE DAWNING OF A NEW DAY

As we have reached the dawning of a new day. What does it look like for you? For you see you are the creator of it. Do you have the vision to create powerful moments each and every day of your life?

Are you ready to stand up and be the change that you've been waiting for? Are you ready to go within, deep within to those places you've been hiding from? Because only there can true change manifest. You have the power to create and manifest the life you want, to live with true purpose, and to be one with your soul. As we heed the calling of a new day, I know you hear the word "Light worker" and you grimace thinking, "Not me! I don't have any special gifts; in fact my life is in shambles." But, I say you are the gift and it is time to stand tall and let your light shine brightly, and to love and embrace yourself completely, as the pure and perfect reflection of God that you are. As your light shines, it will lead the way for another, and together our light will be so bright that no one will be able to deny that a new day has indeed come!

Rev. Dr. Edwige Bingue, Henderson, Nevada
www.affirmationsforliving.net

Author of *You're Not Crazy, You're Awakening: Journey to Discovering Your Soul Purpose, Joy and Abundant Life!*

♥

IS

That one word has become the most powerful tool in my life. When applied consistently, unerringly and unequivocally to everything in existence, it leads to a profound peace, joy, happiness and Love for all of this great creation that is Life.

It took many years of learning and growing before the awareness of IS had begun to seep into my consciousness. The first step was the philosophical learning that all creation is for only one thing, "the healing of God's Son". If the whole purpose of our existence is to learn that we are one Being, the Son part of the Holy Trinity that is God, then every "thing", every "event" in our lives, must fulfill that One purpose.

If God is Love, everything must either be an expression of that Love or a seeking for that Love. If we see anything else, we must be mistaken, be judging incorrectly because we cannot see clearly enough to judge. The next step must be a conscious effort to suspend judgment until we can see clearly enough to know that Love in all things. That is where IS works wonders.

IS… is a complete lack of judgment. It is not modified by words like "good" or "bad", or "right" or "wrong". It stands independently, all by itself. If something just IS, it has no power to disturb my peace. It is not judged as "bad" and therefore doesn't have to become "good" to make me "happy", for I am happy with it as it IS. Nothing is "wrong", and therefore I don't have to be "right" and impose my will on others or on events to make them fit my judgment of what they "should" be.

Likewise, no other person is anything other than the way they are. They can be accepted exactly as IS, without them or anything they do being judged as "right" or "wrong". Then they can be appreciated as they IS, and only the One Son of God appears to my eyes, and I see Love.
IS… isn't a bad definition of Love, unqualified, unconditional positive acceptance?

And then I realized my loving parents gave me the answer to life when I was born. They named me "Denn IS".

Love, IS!!!
Dennis Krum, Las Vegas
Author of IS - Spiritual Insightswww.is1.org

♥

GLIMPSE OF LIGHT

In a world filled with darkness.

It is time to change your mind and the minds of others. Turn around walk or crawl towards the glimpse of light out of the dark tunnel of illusions. To become a brighter more loving individual you.

Make sure you leave deep lasting footprints behind to guide others going through so they may find their way out with support, understanding, encouragement and love.

Know in your mind and heart the sun does shine even in the dark. Just look for that glimpse of light.
Live your life with a heart filled with forgiveness, gratitude, love, openness and Faith.
(Know that your struggles are your strength).
KEEP FAITH & NEVER GIVE UP!!!
Big Healing Hug & God of light love Blessings,

TISH MEZELL, Las Vegas
Author of *Tish Mezell Elactions* (inspirational truth) & *Who Am I*
www.TishMezell.com

♥

PEACE BEGINS WITH ME

Early 2001, I was meditating every day for about an hour at a time. My altar was in the bedroom at the time on top of my dresser. One day, as I was meditating, the lights began to flicker and I was feeling a presence in the room. I kept still, just observing. A few minutes later, my daughter who was 11 at the time, came into my room, sat on my bed next to me, and started crying. I asked her what was wrong. I began to notice they were tears of happiness and joy. She kept telling me that she could feel them. I asked her what she was feeling. She told me that she could feel the angels' wings tickling her face and shoulders. This confirmed that what I was seeing and feeling was not in my mind. We both sat there for many minutes crying. I then asked the angels what message they had for me. They said that I would bring peace to others. I didn't understand what they meant. Was I to go out on a grand scale and promote peace? They didn't answer me, however, I felt such love, peace and joy coming from them.

My mission from that day forward was to bring peace to others. I joined many peace organizations, held peace events, and spoke about peace.

However, as the years went by, I realized that the peace I was to bring to others was that of my own sense of inner peace which they would sense. I didn't have to do anything. It was my own presence that brought them a sense of inner peace.

I adapted Ghandi's popular quote "Be the change you want to see", to "Be the peace you want to see". To obtain inner peace, first begin with meditation every day. Consciously breathe and as you do, inhale while saying to yourself, "I send love and peace to myself" and as you exhale, say, "I send love and peace to others". Each day, bless yourself, others, your food and the animals. Send them all peace and love. Peace can happen one person at a time and it starts with living with inner peace.

Peace and Love,

Mitzi Reed, Las Vegas
Author of Awakening to Your Inner Beauty
www.aspiringconferences.com

♥

EVERY GENIUS IS FIRST THE VILLAGE IDIOT

My Wife was waiting for me at the Door and I will never forget the look on her face, she knew I had just been fired. I was not laid off; in fact I had survived 4 waves of layoffs and with the country in a tail spin economically to keep your job was the main priority for all Americans. I was fired in disgrace for the official reason of "Conflict of interest" and "insubordination". I know big charges, right? In reality I was in the beginning stages of a business idea, I guess you could call a "hobby" something to make a little extra money for my family. An idea called Danny Vegas. In the beginning Danny Vegas was no more than a Las Vegas VIP guy, a private concierge you might say. I have been in customer service for over 25 years, I knew Vegas fairly well so let me create this ultimate Las Vegas insider character and have a go at it. Social media was just getting started but I knew it was a game changer the first time I laid my eyes on it. Social Media would be the way I could get Danny Vegas out of Vegas and introduce him to the whole world. This is so cool. I built a web site and started my efforts on social media. It took time but all was good!

BOOM! BOOM! Out goes the lights!

In September of 2009 the GM of my company got wind of the Danny Vegas world and due to his ignorance and paranoia I was called on the carpet. I had heard through the grapevine I knew he was really studying what I was doing. I heard he was even implying prostitution may be involved. On September 14th I was called in and suspended and told to take Danny Vegas Down or get sent down the road. Thinking back I wish I could tell you I stuck it to the man and defied his order and kept my little hobby going and triumphed. No I had a family I needed to take care of. My head said one thing but my heart said another. I called my web company and took down my website. Danny Vegas was dead before he really got started. The reality is just because you take your website down in real time doesn't mean your website comes off the internet in real time. On September 19th a company Google search found Danny Vegas alive and well on the internet. I was fired two hours later. When I returned home my wife was at the door with a look on her face I will never forget, it was truly, at the time, the worst day of my life. The country in a severe recession, no jobs to be had and I just lost mine due to a stupid hobby because of a character that in reality did not even exist.

Fast Forward

If you thought this story is about never giving up and fighting through hard times to live a dream you would be right! There were no jobs to be had and I knew if I found a job the pay would be dismal. I revived Danny Vegas and I put the website back up. I tweaked the plan, I got rid of what did not work and kept what people wanted. The road was long and the family suffered. My relationship with my wife suffered. I was so close to quitting so many times I can't even tell you how many. For the first two years, The Danny Vegas brand did not make a dime. In fact, the business lost money and with a family of four living on one income of less than $40,000.00 a year to say the least there was stress and huge tension. Why I did not give up, I don't know. My wife did not deserve this, my kids went without many things that most kids had. We shopped in thrift stores for clothes and bought our food at the 99 cent stores. In reality we were poor, and my family was living in poverty but I would not quit Danny Vegas and something drove me on.

Today we are a million dollar company! Hell no, but Danny Vegas makes a living and is growing every day. We have sponsors and great media partners. The Danny Vegas brand is established in the Las Vegas Community and has fans all over the world. The Brand is respected and doors open wherever the company goes. The Company has created jobs and works with charities all over the Las Vegas Valley. All of us at Danny Vegas work hard every day to move forward and be a force for good. Remember, every genius is at first the village idiot. Keep Rocking!

Danny Vegas, Las Vegas
www.dannyvegaslive.com

♥

WHAT WOULD A WORLD WITHOUT VIOLENCE AND FEAR LOOK LIKE?

I believe it would look like a garden. A beautiful garden birthed by the universe and kissed by the sun. It would be a place where abundance is the norm, not the exception, a place where the rivers dance, songs are sung and love is given without conditions. It would be a place where mountains stand strong and waves of green and gold dance in the wind across the prairies. It would look like you. It would look like me. It would look like our world today.

When you hear of violent acts or face troubles in your life, you may wonder what is happening. Where has peace and kindness gone?

I dare to say that you do not need to find peace. It is not lost.

Peace is here, in the garden of the earth, whispering to your soul. It whispers – "Pay attention. Remember who you are".

You are a part of the earth's garden, and she needs you to remember your connection to spirit. Sit quietly and allow peace to reveal itself to you.

When this happens, there is no more room for anger or fear - only peace and kindness can take root and bloom.

So go now and sit quietly in life's garden. Let the earth's tapestry wrap you in the peace that is the birthright of all things belonging to the creator. Let the plants and animals honor you with their presence – they have not forgotten. Listen to their conversations. Become one with all of God's creations and you will know peace. It is here, now, waiting for you to remember.

Jamie Lee, Las Vegas

♥

SOUL CALLS FOR HOME

There are some of you feeling haunted by your past as you exist in this world. You walk through life half awake and half present, searching for something to feed your soul. Yet, you feel as if you are overwhelmed by two worlds. A world of who you think you are and a world of completeness within your spirit.

Your spirit encompasses other humans upon earth who reflect all that you know. Earth, known as the third dimensional plane, is where you possess a potent factor – will. The will to maintain focus towards the destination reveals your truth. It is never about the arrival, only about the beginning. Your purpose has come full circle towards something massive within the planetary grid.

As you are aroused, you will no longer wish to be within the physical stature of humanness. The body must not be allowed to dictate its limitations to your soul. The soul must rule the body, because the soul is neither caused by nor dependent on the body. In the soul's will lies all power. We must realize that energy and will go together. It is a very simple formula. We have been so conditioned to the idea that energy comes only from material sources that we fail to believe in and draw upon the cosmic source, which responds instantly to will.

Take a moment and open your eyes to watch the universe play out your life like a movie. It portrays your authentic self through love. Love is the master of our soul; feel your heart being awakened by God with an unspoken promise.

Soul is pro-actively accessing and enriching our subconscious mind through the five human sensory gateways (sight, sound, taste, touch and smell), opening up our intuition through synchronicity of the law of the universe. But we must first connect to our voice of truth to fulfill our duties of purpose, no longer being silent. It begins with opening our sense of sight to live our spiritual path-sharing with others. Your soul-my soul-becomes ravenous to be home again.

When we are in tuned with the universal laws, our soul initiates a transmutation between spirit and human consciousness, merging as one. We have all been the observer and it is time to cultivate our wholeness. We each are masters of what we have learned about self through our thoughts and feelings.

Surrendering to divine guidance is evidentiary proof of the totality of our existence. We no longer are repetitious in creating the same results in our life, but we are evolving as higher vibration to cease what does not serve us.

We are not subservient to the lower energies within our physical body. We have prepared ourselves to go deep within to awaken our soul to unite with our divine creator.

Charmaine Lee, Las Vegas
www.foundationforinsight.com
Author of *Gardenias Bruise Easily*

♥

SECURE YOUR MASK FIRST

There are moments in your life, when you hear a phrase said so many times, and one day... you actually *hear* it.

I was traveling on a long flight back to Las Vegas from Korea. The safety video was playing. As usual, most the passengers were not paying attention. On this particular flight, I happened to be seated in the emergency row. I felt like it was my civic duty to pay somewhat attention to the safety video, in case I needed to rescue hundreds of passengers and ultimately end up on national news talking about my heroic actions. Sometimes it's good to daydream.

The safety video goes on to play the oxygen mask scene, demonstrating what to do in the event that the masks are needed. The classic video shows the masks drop in front of a way-too-calm mother and her 6-year old son. The narrator goes on to state:

"Secure your mask first, before helping someone else with their mask."

Those words, I've heard time and time again, on every flight I've taken. On that day, I heard it differently. It occurred to me that this statement is true in money, time and love.

Think of it this way, you have a cup and a saucer. The cup starts out full... full of your money, time and love. You give a little money to your brother who only needs $500 to have his car fixed; the liquid in your cup goes down. Then a friend needs you to help run some errands for them even though you are slammed at work, the liquid goes down even more. Now overwhelmed and stressed out, you are feeling guilty that you are not spending enough time with your husband. You run around attempting to have a nice dinner prepared for him. Your cup is now nearly empty and you are about to have a nervous breakdown.

Life is demanding. Yes. I get it. I've been there, many times. What I know for sure is the only way to get back to having more energy and feeling good is to *put your oxygen mask on first* and to *fill your cup up first*. This is a reminder to be good to you. Take time for yourself. Ensure you have a healthy financial. Above all else, love yourself first.

When your cup is overfilled because you took care of yourself first, your cup will overflow into the saucer... and *this* is what you can afford to give away.

"Secure your mask first, before helping anyone with their mask."

In other words, "Secure your *money, time* and *love* first, before helping someone else with their *money, time* and *love*."

Tammy Shaw-Grabel, Las Vegas
www.lvwomanmagazine.com

♥

WELCOME TO MY WORLD

I grew up listening to a lot of Country Music, and one song that often runs through my head is 'Welcome to My World' recorded by Jim Reeves. The particular lyric that inspires me most is: "Knock and the door will open, seek and you will find, ask and you'll be given – the key to this world of mine." Utilizing biblical wisdom in a love song provides an interesting twist. This song always reminds me that if I don't like what I see around me, then I should pay attention to what I am seeking.

I often sense a deeper meaning within the lyrics of a song. "Welcome to My World" was written as a love song, but for me, it is a message from "universal consciousness", welcoming me into a world of awareness and loving vibration. For instance, I always find what I am seeking. When I look for tragedy, I find it in abundance. When I look for hope, I find that in abundance. When I ask the universe for wisdom, clarity, and assistance, it is always given. When I knock on the doors of enlightenment and guidance, they are always opened.

I suppose it shouldn't surprise me to find such wisdom

in popular songs. After all, I strive to see the divine in everything. Why shouldn't Spirit inspire an artist to share profound wisdom wrapped within a catchy tune, or movie, or TV show? I grew up hearing that "God works in mysterious ways." The longer I live, the more I understand the depth of that statement.

Whatever your life looks like at this particular moment, it can shift in an instant. What you see next will depend on what you are seeking. What are you looking for? Are you looking for evidence of peace, joy, and abundance? Are you asking Spirit to guide you? Are you open to the possibility? Are you knocking on the door of divine abundance?

Shift your vision toward the things that you desire. Move in the direction of your dreams, always looking for what will serve your journey. Give no energy to the distractions that would take you down a path of heartache and despair. Trust me, if you sincerely desire to see the divine, you will find it all around you – "waiting just for you, welcome to my world."

"Welcome to my World
(written by Jesse Collins and Kenny Blank)

Welcome to my world
Won't you come on in?
Miracles I guess

Still happen now and then

Step into my heart
Leave your cares behind
Welcome to my world
Built with you in mind

Knock and the door will open
Seek and you will find
Ask and you'll be given
The key to this world of mine

I'll be waiting here
With my arms unfurled
Waiting just for you
Welcome to my world.

Susan M. Wright, Pahrump Nevada
www.beacon-of-life.com
Author of *Putting Down the Paddles: 30 Days to Living in the Flow*

♥

WITH LOVE IN YOUR HEART
YOU WILL GET PEACE

"Peace," means feelings of tranquility, mental calm, and serenity, a warm tender affection for others is produced. When the body feels peaceful the brain chemical dopamine is released and this gives you feelings of well-being and altruism, which is concern for others. When your heart is full of love for oneself and others maladaptive behavior, criminality, envy, jealously, prejudice, and racism will be obliterated and is replaced with feelings of peace, tranquility, and well-being. Just think if you had a day in which all you felt was love, you would be at peace. It would be as if you were walking along the seashore, feeling sprinkles of water from the waves misty on your face, or hiking up a mountainous path, smelling the beautiful pine trees, jasmine blossoms, and eucalyptus trees. In your own neighborhood, you can listen to the children playing in the park, birds chirping, smelling the flowers, listening to the neighbor playing "Moonlight Sonata," on the piano; watching the high school band practicing on the field, playing an R&B song jamming all the way, sunbathing by the pool sipping a caramel

Frappuccino, and soaking in vitamin D from the rays of the illustrious sun. Peace is what we need and we can get there in the simplest of ways.

Patricia Brown, Las Vegas
www.authorpatriciabrown.com
Author of *Nine Lives of a Baby Boomer*

♥

LOVE IS THE ONLY POWER

My dear friend Gwen transitioned back to her maker at age forty-nine. It was a slow and horrible suicide; she died of liver failure—drinking volumes of vodka a day for the past four years. Gwen was wonderfully loveable when she was sober. That's how I met her in May 2005. She had only been ninety days sober, but I didn't know. She was amazing and so funny. My husband John, Gwen and I chatted over dinner for hours as though we had a friendship for a thousand years. She was a sophisticated, 5'10, voluptuous blonde with hazel green eyes.

Our friendship was spawned out of work in self-development. We learned, served, and coached others together. Gwen had oodles of parties at her beautiful home in the country club. She brought so much joy to others. When Gwen called, we ran to her. I cared deeply for her and our friendship. We nicknamed her Mama Gwen because she was just that for so many of us. Yet somewhere in her deepest core, she couldn't feel our love.

Gwen relapsed in February 2008, after slashing her

hand from broken glass while trying to clean a fish bowl. The dirty fish water caused unknown bacteria to painfully grow up her arm. It was the pain killers she was given to help after her surgery that started it all again. Gwen turned into a foul, malicious drunk. She was self-loathing, believing that no one ever loved her and that she was only used for the things she had and did for others. She would lash out at those who loved and adored her. We were all at a loss.

My beloved friend, who felt abandoned by John and I (and many others), hated me for not accepting her and loving her as a drunk. She passed with the feelings of abandonment and lovelessness. As I sat there in Hospice holding and gently rubbing her hand and talking to her, I realized she had abandoned herself. She could never feel the love of her husband, her fifteen year old son, her girlfriends, her employees or anyone else for that matter. Here was this powerfully driven woman who just needed to fall in love with herself.

As I reflect on my own 45 years of life I realize that most of us have some self-loathing. What ways can I be in relationship with me and fall madly in love with me? How do I choose to spend my next 25 years? Do I choose to slowly eat myself to death and allow my body to fall apart with harmful foods? Do I surround myself with toxic people and dramas? Or do I choose to use discernment and surround myself with love? How much do I truly love myself? *Love is the only power.* We want it. We seek it. We sing about it, write about it, and make movies about it. But it's always right inside, crying to be awakened.

Catherine Ormand, Henderson Nevada
Catherine@drormand.com

♥

THE ROAD TO SUCCESS

Success is available to anyone willing to do whatever it takes to overcome the challenges that most often gets in the way of any worthwhile achievement. Applying enough persistence and determination is the key to conquering any challenge. Simply stated, if we do the things that make people succeed, we will succeed and if we do the things that make people fail, we will fail.

Total Success is divided into 4 areas:
1. Emotional Success
2. Mental Success
3. Financial Success
4. Spiritual Success

Emotional Success is achieving mastery in unconditional love and happiness. Emotional Success is revealed through our family and friend relationships.

Emotional Success is a complete and total forgiveness and acceptance of yourself and/or anybody else needing forgiveness. Emotional Success is the compassion to realize that no one is defective and that everyone is doing their best within their circumstance, beliefs and education.

Mental Success is achieving mastery in Know-how, Intelligence and Intuition.

Mental Success is the realization that Life has an unerring way of putting us in the perfect situations and circumstances necessary for our growth and development into higher states of consciousness. Mental Success causes the revelation that Life is our greatest teacher, always sending feedback messages. For example, if we don't like the results, Life is telling us that we need to change how we are going about it. For this reason, *there is no such thing as failure, only feedback.*

Financial Success is achieving Abundance and Prosperity consciousness. Prosperity and Abundance consciousness is the realization that scarcity, lack and limitations are only self-created illusions. Our truthful reality is we have more air than we can breathe, more water than we can drink, more people than we can meet or more places than we can go. Financial Success is a realization that it's not the money that we really want but it's the things that money can buy. Long lasting Financial Success results from impeccable integrity in all business dealings. 2 important things to remember for achieving Financial Success are:

1. Keep it Simple
2. Money is Attracted to Good Ideas

Spiritual Success is achieving Perfect Health, Higher States of Consciousness and Divine Wisdom

Spiritual Success is our Soul becoming awake into the unbounded power, infinite and eternal nature of the 'I Am Presence.' Spiritual Success turns our problems into an opportunity to reveal our level of consciousness. Proper Nutrition and Exercise, Cleansing and Purification are the ways to Spiritual Success. Practicing daily Meditation in addition to proper sleep accelerates the process of attaining Spiritual Success. Divine Wisdom is the realization that 'We cannot control everything, but we can control our response to anything' and how we respond to things that happen reveals our level of maturity and Spiritual Success.

Right action will advance us closer to or even beyond our goals.
Eternal Blessings

Reverend Thabiti, Las Vegas
ThePower.com
Author of the books, *All about You*, *The 52 Illuminations* and *The Secret Wisdom of the Ages*

♥

RECIPE FOR DREAM STEW (PLUS DESSERT)

The quickest way to create something new is to accept that you don't know everything and to know that *you don't have to.*

Say whaaa? Yeah, I said it.

Not knowing + accepting that we don't know = allowing.

Allowing = ever so necessary aspect of the creation process we tend to forget (because we want it NOW [cue foot stomping]).

Reminder: Instant gratification is only satisfying to the mind. Drugs, Facebook, and cutting all fall into this category (and are things I have overcome [okay maybe not Facebook, but I've gotten a lot better!]).

When we say, "I don't know, *but I want to.*"

Or

"This totally sucks, *but it doesn't have to.*"

We bring an element of possibility to otherwise conclusive statements-a spark of hope during those moments of doubt and hopelessness that come with the territory of being human.

Yay! We're human! Dance party!

When we honor the absolute truth of who we are and

what we are experiencing RIGHT NOW, *then* add our desires, we give them a lot more oomph and plenty of legroom to fill us up in ways we didn't know was possible. Feel the sense of relief this statement offers:

You don't have to know everything. Each step you take with your biggest, most glorious intentions in your heart brings your dreams closer to you. The more you clarify who you've decided you want to be and which part you'd like to play, the easier it will be for your dreams to find you.

By way of your thoughts.

By way of your feelings.

By way of places you go, people you meet, dreams you awaken from.

And nudges you feel.

How do you feel now?

To really magnify and ground the frequency you're now emitting, I'd like for you to join me in a journaling exercise.

JOURNAL TIME! (Think: MC Hammer)

If you've got a journal, awesome (I love you). If not (I love you too), any piece of paper lined or unlined will do.

On the blank page, write down and answer the following questions:

Who do I want to be?

And

What can I do to be more authentically, wonderfully, imperfectly me?

When you're finished writing, breathe in what you've written.

Deeply.

Congratulations! Your answers have brought you in alignment with your dreams and desires. You can now take either itty-bitty steps or some giant leaps toward your goals (you know what to do). Whichever you prefer. The actions you take *must* be in alignment with who you are and the wonderful, ever so fulfilling work you were born to do. If you're all human doing and no human being, you're likely to face plant frequently.

Which is totally fine, but I prefer not to face plant it.

I'd rather live it.

And love it.

The bumps and bruises along the way are there to show you it's time to look within and start asking the right questions.

The ones that, when you answer, make you say and feel and know,

"I HAVE PURPOSE!"

Your dreams are within reach when you reach within first.

Things to remember (for me too)

1. No one can ever be better at being you, thank you. You are awesome at it.

2. Make a decision. You'll get where you're going as long as you keep moving.

3. Label your feelings. For example, say, "I'm frustrated. Okay. Cool. So now what?" Once you know where you're at, you can easily decide where you'd like to go from there.

I'll leave you with a fun process that I created (with the help of the creative power and imagination of my beloved two year old, Adin). This is a little game you can play to make life easier.

First, answer this question:

In a single word, what is the one thing you feel you're missing that would make you feel whole again?

Once you've identified the word, using your hands, form it into an imaginary pie that fits in the palm of your hand. As you do so, say something like, "I am making a delicious, delectable, delightful _____ (your word) pie. It is going to provide me with exactly what I need."

When you feel it is complete, eat your energetic pie and feel the difference!

(I made and ate a confidence pie just now. Nom.)

If you are already feeling whole and grand right now, you can always make a love pie. Or an appreciation pie. You can never have too much of those.

That creative, playful part of you is just that.

Creative

Confident

And pretty darn cool

Have fun!

With love pie, Carrie Leigh Sandoval, North Las Vegas
www.carrieleighsandoval.com
Author of *Journals Have Feelings Too: A Guidebook for Writing and Your Way Back to Sanity*

♥

LETTING GO OF GUILT

How often have we thought of something that we have done or not done over the past week and felt a pang of Guilt? You know, the phone call we didn't return, the evening we spent watching TV rather than doing the laundry (or cleaning out that closet, or writing Christmas cards, or ???) Or perhaps focusing on the bill that didn't get paid on time, or...

How does that feeling of guilt serve us? Some might say that feeling guilty motivates us to do better next time. But does it? I suggest that guilty feelings actually do us harm. When we don't feel good about ourselves, do we usually make changes, or have the energy to do what we have put off? Rarely, if ever.

Instead, we will have a piece of chocolate, or zone in front of the TV, or chat on Facebook, have a glass of wine or a beer, or distract ourselves in some way. Why do we feel the need for distraction? Because we are feeling lousy about ourselves. When we feel guilty, we are feeling like we don't deserve what we want in life, that we are not worthy of respect, or love or approval. We feel like we have failed in some way.

I believe that when we perpetuate these feelings, by choosing to feel guilty (yes, it is a choice!), we are "dimming the light" of who we really are. We are depleting our own energy, we are lowering our vibration. From the perspective of the Law of Attraction, we are moving further away from realizing all that we want and desire in life.

So, does Guilt really benefit us? NO! When we feel guilty and tell ourselves that we are bad, we are not motivated to do it differently next time, we usually just try and distract ourselves from feeling bad. What DOES sometimes happen, is that if we don't feel great about our past choices, we can make different choices that WILL make us feel better. Change only occurs when we have forgiven ourselves for our "imperfection" (who said we are supposed to be perfect anyhow?), and we want to do something that makes us feel good about ourselves.

I am suggesting that imposing Guilt on ourselves just prolongs the misery, encourages us to procrastinate, and not change. What really motivates us is when we feel good? When we look at ourselves in the mirror and see someone that we like, respect – even love?

How would life be different if we lightened up on ourselves? What if when we make a mistake, we say "Oops!", immediately forgive ourselves and move forward? Would we not have more energy? Would we not be kinder and more loving to ourselves? And, if we are more loving to ourselves, won't we have more love to give? All this, by simply choosing to let go of Guilt.

Maureen Pua'ena O'Shaughnessy, Las Vegas & Hawaii
www.InJoyingLife.com

Author of *My Naked Journey: A Reiki Master's Quest to Live Authentically*

♥

IMAGINE

Enjoying your unique beauty in the face of every woman you meet
Wishing ALL people well, no matter the circumstances
Expecting and manifesting kindness hourly
Healthiness and vitality
Equality for ALL
Not seeing people as having or being more or less
Happiness and contentment
Using your good experiences to teach and enlighten
Being proud of every one you know
Being proud without arrogance
Not comparing your lifestyle to that of anyone else
Seeing your fears and disappointments as lessons, and moving forward anyway
Visualizing people as their greater selves
When we realize that our unique gifts and contributions are equally valuable, not be compared to, or measured against, we will then accept and lift each other up daily.

Xena Foreman, Las Vegas
www.facebook.com/xcccssorizeyourlife

♥

LAS VEGAS-SHE WILL
SPEAK TO YOU

A touchstone in my experience of living in Las Vegas has been a particularly vivid dream which I had one night after attending a spiritual gathering at a friend's home near Red Rock. In the dream, an encompassing Feminine presence spoke in a woman's voice. She seemed to be emanating from the desert basin of which Vegas is a part. The basin appeared as salty, sparkling and crystalline, a womb like ancient ocean floor sans water. I was enveloped by a sense of calming depth.

"You will come fully into your womanhood here," the Feminine presence told me, as I surveyed the phosphorescent moonlit beauty that surrounded me.

That dream took place about nine years ago, not long after I had moved to Las Vegas from Los Angeles.

As promised by the Feminine presence in that initiatory dream, Las Vegas has indeed been a crucible and a witness of my coming into and embracing my womanhood. This place is where my deepest relationships abide. It is where my most profound experiences of desire and loss and love and betrayal have taken root.

Vegas is also where I've become acutely aware of how the Feminine is denied, threatened and denigrated.

There truly exists a Dirty Vegas that is a dumping ground and a receptacle of the abject fantasies of those who cannot hear Her voice.

Apocalypse rehearsals, chemtrails, child sex trafficking, the agonies of the discarded homeless and indigenous, and nuclear genocide leave an indelible stain here. The intent to obliterate life is recorded in the Nevada desert — part of a glistening expanse that only seems barren of memory.

I've come to view the hyper-masculine forms and institutions associated with Vegas — the mafia, the winner-takes-all mentality that devastates the vulnerable, the casino culture that sets up women as trophies, the idea that there should be no consequences for whatever one does to someone else sexually — as unskilled, unconscious reactions to a profoundly Feminine and antithetical presence that resides here.

The challenge in Vegas — as in many places — is to disengage from the use of feminine energy to support a worldview and economy in which authentic Feminine presence is denied. To UN-identify with the stock female bodies conflated with plastic objects on billboards, to reject lethal and addictive alcoholic feminine energy substitutes, to relinquish the ideal of the sex worker who delivers erotic releases with mechanical efficiency.

The Feminine presence which resides here is much deeper, more secure and more ancient than the history of organized crime, than the violence against the bodies and souls of women, than the legacy of female dismemberment and abduction that have become synonymous with the dark economy of Vegas.

The challenge is to *not* replace or forsake the essential Feminine. Not to fear Her. Not to shun Her because She is an authentic source of life energy that makes our pursuit of substitutes seem cheap and shallow in comparison.

Seek Her beneath and beyond the fluorescent and neon glare. She will speak to you if you allow Her to.

Lynn Boland, Las Vegas
www.facebook.com/lynn.boland.56

♥

CREATING TRUE HEARTFELT HAPPINESS

"Dearest Light worker, Adult Indigo and Earth Angel, We see you so often wondering about your life purpose, searching for it amid more job applications and interviews, only to take jobs and careers that only half fulfill you.

To you we say, have patience. The steps you took in the past were not the wrong ones; they were perfect for the time being.

As the planet continues its ascending know that many wonderful new developments will take place. It is important to keep your heart open and activate it during meditations to listen to its calling.

Furthermore, do not disregard the emotions that come during your menses and at other regular times in the month for men. Move into the heart and learn to listen to your needs and pray to receive guidance to *have a life that merits true heartfelt happiness.*

We see some of you beginning to move into the heart space and become increasingly aware of what could be different, longing for a community of conscious happy souls.

The present world economies reflect the outdated root chakra energies of separating and organizing for safety and flow while the heart believes in communities and co-partnerships and co-operation. A new heart-based economy is beginning to emerge and will succeed if each of you listen to your own needs and pray to be guided to take inspired actions.

The meditation we would like to do with you now is to help you open up your ear Chakras so you can listen to your heart calling and the angel's answers to your prayers. Please practice it for at least seven days keeping a journal and pen nearby throughout the day paying special attention to new ideas you receive spontaneously or during your meditations.

Meditation:

As you read this you can actually keep your eyes open or close them at the end of each line. Try it both ways and see what works for you.

1. Imagine two white robbed angels with bright light all around their aura and hands.

2. Imagine the angels on either side of you are sending

light into your heart center from their happy smiling heart.

4. Can you breathe in that light, feel it coming into your heart from the outside in?

5. Finally exhale through your nose and imagine the light traveling up to be released through your ears.

6. And again inhale light into your heart from the angel's light. Let it travel into your heart and when you exhale let it pass up to your nose imagining air + light is being pushed up to your ears.

7. You may feel a need to shake your head and release trapped energies out of your ears.

8. Repeat for at least 10 breaths or more.

With each breath you breathe in, you are breathing in light. With each exhale you are imagining the air + light exiting from the ears.

If you feel one ear more blocked than the other, bring your conscious focus to that ear and say to it:

"Whatever is causing this block, I am now ready to release you. I ask all powerful spirit/god/angels to resolve the situation completely. I am ready to hear the truth and take inspired actions daily to create a meaningful heart centered life."

As an intuitive soul, you deserve to have all channels of communication open.

Danielle Dove, Las Vegas
www.danielledove.com
www.healingdovetherapy.com
Author of *Creating Sacred Spaces, Earth Angels in Training, Living Goddess Guide + Journal* and *Healing Dove Therapy*

♥

JUST HOLD ON

Just wait. Hold on for one more second. Just stay for a while longer because someone here needs you.

You act like everything is fine. You laugh at people's jokes; you do goofy things with your friends and act like you have a carefree life. But when you come home, you just turn off that mental switch. Then suddenly, you break down. You feel alone, empty and tired. You can't seem to put into words how you feel; there are two sides of you. The one you show people and the part of you, you hide from the world.

The screaming gets louder. The hitting gets harder. The bruises get darker. The scars get deeper. And eventually you get lonelier. But there will be a day when the screaming turns into silence. The hitting no longer exists. The bruises will fade away. The scars heal. And you will no longer be alone because the one that needed you will have you.

The weight of the world just falls upon your shoulders; and you can't help it. You feel like no one is around to help you or let alone understand you. You are always vulnerable and you are never at peace. The world is a cruel place. But there is good that lives in the bad, and bad that grows into the good. So, ignore the bad and seek out the good, then the weight of the world will be lifted off your shoulders. The raging tides will become gentle waves; the fierce fires will become just a flame. The heavy rocks will become dust; and the trees will no longer fall but instead stand tall.

The world is not an easy place to stay, but it has so much to offer: love and laughter, peace and joy. Even in the darkness you can always find the light. You are never alone in this world.

Wait for the good moments in life. Like those mosh pits of butterflies you get in your stomach around your first crush. The careless feeling you get when you go to a concert. When you overcome the fear you've held onto for all these years. The moment on your 80th birthday you look back and reflect at what an amazing life you've had. These moments are worth living for.

Let go of the past; that time was dark and lonely. Let go of the tears, screams and pain. Face and overcome the fear of your past, present and future. The nightmares will fade away into the darkness. Nothing will hold you down; you can be free. But, you have to be strong and take it into your hands.

You see…taking your life does not end the bad situations; it eliminates all the good possibilities in life. Yes, the world is a cruel place but it supplies the loving moments that can occur. So, ignore that hateful voice in the back of your head. You are beautiful, lovely, wonderful and precious. The world wouldn't be the same without you. Just hold on a little while longer.

Nalani Malia Paliotta, Las Vegas
15 years old

♥

MEMO:
YOUR COUNTRY NEEDS YOU.

To Love the Enemy and Save the World
Imagine if you received a memo like this.

Would you be up for the challenge? Would your super-hero curiosity be piqued? Mine certainly would be. I'd be looking for my cape and getting ready for some fearless maneuvers!

Granted, we don't usually receive such notes calling for grand gestures to save the world. But there is a plethora of daily opportunities to transform the lives of those around us through acts of kindness, compassion and love.

And so today, as you read this, I want us to use our most human attribute: our consciousness to create world peace... beginning with ourselves.

We are going to send love to those we have deemed un-worthy of our love for any reason. For example, someone who has caused us deep harm, abandoned us, or some-one we just "don't like". (Keep in mind - animosity never appears out of thin air. There's always a reason for such strong feelings).

You may be asking yourself, "Why should I do that? Those people owe me. They have hurt me."

The purpose of this exercise is to *expand our capacity for love and to radiate peace*. We must transcend our histories of hurt, and whomever we've labeled as the "enemy" responsible. By stretching our compassion muscles in these particularly challenging areas, we can begin to contemplate the possibility of inner and world peace.

Will you answer the call?
Here we go. And thank you.

Find an amazing spot to sit for this mediation. Begin to become aware of your breath, and consciously allow external distractions to slip away from your mind and body. Take another deep breath, and close your eyes.

Now, think of someone you don't like, or feel angry with, or deem unworthy of your love. Take the first person who comes into your awareness, and allow them to stand to the right of you in your consciousness.

Turn your attention back to yourself. Breathe, and remain in the stillness you've created. When you are ready, ask your body where it holds the ability or quality of love that can transcend fear, judgment, or your own story of being hurt.

86

Take your awareness to the place that holds this expansive, transcendent capacity to love. What does it feel like? Is it warm or light? Allow your senses to touch and vibrate with this energy. Once you can feel its presence vibrating through your body, begin to radiate it out as waves of energy towards your "enemy".

Observe what happens. Does the person move away or change? Stay focused on being in this experience of transcendent love, allowing it to flow freely from you. Take your time to deeply connect to this energy, and the healing transformation that is taking place. Let your mind be silent. Continue in this exercise until the person leaves, or fades into the light.

Now, take another deep breath, and begin to radiate this loving energy into yourself - into all the places you hold judgment against you, or feel unworthy. Allow the same wonderful, transcendent energy to pour into your inner fibers, nourishing and healing you. Take as long as you like, or until you feel you have completed this transformation.

As we clear the energy fields within our own bodies and auras, we have our first taste of peace, acceptance, love for ourselves and those we deem our enemies.
Yippee! Let's get it on!

Navjit Kandola, Las Vegas/United States
www.TenderLogic.com

♥

REMEMBERING LOVE

Many of you feel alone. This could not be further from the truth. You are part of a collective whole that consists of pure, unconditional love. You have simply forgotten who you are and where you came from.

There is inside of you, right now, the memory of your true identity, and your true place in the cosmos. Your essence, your consciousness, is in every particle of matter and energy in the universe. You are simply choosing to focus on the piece that is the human identity you see in the mirror.

You cannot be separate from the universal whole. You can only forget your connection, but you cannot sever it. If you sit in silence, you will hear the tone of Oneness. If you look inside your heart you will remember the connection you have with all. You must push away the vibrations that disrupt your memory. These are fear, anxiety, shame, guilt, anger, and sadness. These vibrations pull you away from your memories.

Lift yourself to joy, compassion, and gratitude and the memories of your connection to Love will resurface.

When you feel alone, sit in silence. Forget all that you struggle with, and remember only where you come from. From Love. Let this memory refill your soul. When your cup is empty, you have but to refill it in the ocean of Love. This ocean is always present, is always now, and cannot be depleted.

There is nothing in the world that is not part of you. Where you see struggle, darkness, and fear, you are seeing spots where someone is blocking themselves from receiving and remembering love. Change your vibration to change theirs, for you cannot change their vibration without first adjusting yours.

You cannot see it with your eyes, but every single one of you is holding hands with everyone else. Walk together. Share the joy of the journey. Share the memory of love with those who are forgetting. Hold them tenderly. Do not judge, do not reject. In every person is your essence too.

When you have forgotten... when you feel alone... go back to the memory of unconditional love. It is in your heart. Feel the energy of love coming into your being, and remember that it is impossible to lose this connection. You walk with many. And you are never truly alone.

Erin Pavlina, Las Vegas
www.erinpavlina.com
Author of the *Astral Projection Guidebook: Mastering the Art of Astral Travel*

♥

HIDDEN SECRETS

Las Vegas commonly referred to as Sin City, is the playground known for all types of destruction. I moved to Las Vegas in 1986, and my life has never been the same. One of the greatest hidden secrets of Vegas is about the residents that make up this great city.

What isn't listed on the LVAC, what isn't printed on the billboards that overlook this fabulous Glitter Gulch of lights and fantasy, is the wonderful community of hard working and faith-based individuals that reside here. This is the city I was destined to know, and the place that would define my life in Christ.

I remember the solemn times through my years of growing, times when I heard His whispers. Where did the whispers come from? Out of nowhere, like the wind that blew against my skin, the sound of whispering would blow across my soul. A quiet voice saying the most beautiful things, the feeling of peace and calm would enfold me, telling me of things I had no understanding of. This must be the spirit of the Lord, who else would want me to hear such, and feel the presence of joy, peace, and love. Why me?

God grants us his grace to walk through the storms, his blessings to uplift us through hard times, the opportunity for us to grow in faith. The life of a believer will be filled with trials. The Lord does not allow storms in our lives to destroy us, but to change our direction, strengthen us, and build our character. The intention for our trials is that we learn to seek Him and find our hope and trust in Him. Where broken fences once stood in our lives, God has mended our hearts.

Regardless of what faith you come from, which religion, or not, that you decide to follow there lays a world of hope for those looking for something to believe in. Multitudes of inspiring people can help bring your hopes and dreams into a reality. A base of interfaith churches and ministries can bring the love of God into personal and family relationships.

As a Christian I can honestly say, there is no place like Las Vegas. A place where entrepreneurs thrive, where prayer is reflected, where the heart searches for goodness, where love oversees, and where we wholeheartedly seek revelation for direction.

A life of health, wellness and faith can be found in the land of the desert, and the city of entertainment.

Victorya Campe, Las Vegas
www.messagesoffaith.net
Author of *Chosen, 15 Minutes with Jesus*

♥

I WOULD LOVE TO SPEND MY LIFE COLLECTING SUNSETS

I will carry with me always these brilliant images brim-
ming with the deepest reds, yellows, violets and indigos,
given to all of us as a gift from Divine Source.
I would then have a life filled with vibrant tapestries
woven in golden threads of sunlight and dusk.
And when I leave this world I will take with me my
collection of Sunsets.
These mosaics of love and light are now and forever
more imbued into my cells and engraved into my very
marrow and bones.
They shall travel with me and continue to fill my heart
with
joy for all Eternity.
I am Serene and filled with Peace.
And so it is.

Barbara Berg, Las Vegas
Author of *Desert Dreamers* a bath book for healing the
soul

♥

4 PRINCIPLES FOR A HAPPY, FULFILLED LIFE

I am a Reiki Master-Teacher, light worker and healer. Reiki is my passion and life. As a child I desired to "fix" difficult situations, relationship problems, and people. I lacked proper tools then, but now, with Reiki energy healing, I help others, on their spiritual path, and with everyday stresses, hurts, and losses we all face. I've experienced miraculous changes in myself and others, and I am grateful to God and the Universe for the abundance and prosperity that is available for the asking.

I consider the following four principles vital to a happy, fulfilled life for all people: healers or not.

1. Self-nurturing. Light workers, caretakers, and lay people lose sight of this important aspect. We take well-being, and health for granted, as we give to people we love. But without nourishing ourselves, in whatever healthy manner needed, we become drained on physical and emotional levels. All we give to others, we must also give to ourselves. From a power nap, a hot bath, personal time to meditate, relax, or eat healthy, it's imperative to keep

ourselves strong to give quality time, love and emotion to others. It's simple; your car can't run without gas, and your body can't run on depleted energy. You can't give what you don't have!

2. Ego. Reiki teaches us to get ego out of the way. As Practitioners we channel energy from the Universe to the recipient. The results are relaxation, stress and pain relief, emotional breakthroughs, and downright healing miracles on a physical, emotional or spiritual level. Yes we help people heal, but we must prevent a distorted view of our own ego, or power. In any person's life, no matter their profession or calling, balance is needed. Ego can motivate, or ego can destroy. Spiritual wholeness cannot exist where ego resides.

3. Discernment. Some people have no common sense; others have poor discernment. There comes a time when a person must rely on gut instincts, what their heart knows, or what they know is right, through knowledge, life experience, or the good or bad energy they feel. Good choices come from good discernment.

4. Exemplary life. By that I simply mean, walk your talk. If you preach something, be it! If you want love, respect, abundance, prosperity, honesty, or peace of mind; you must possess those qualities. If you say you're a loving, compassionate person, then be one. If you expect honesty and respect, show those qualities in your everyday actions. We can teach more, and help more people, by living what we say we are.

Sarah Michaels, Las Vegas, NV
Author of *Children's Motivational Stories, Romance And Technical Works*

♥

IF CHILDREN CAN DO THIS, WE ADULTS CAN TOO-PEACE BEGINS WITH ME

Ever since my earlier career as a Montessori teacher, I have been captivated by the vision and peace philosophy of pioneering educator, Dr. Maria Montessori. Long before she partnered with her contemporary Mahatma Gandhi, Montessori advocated a peaceful revolution in humanity beginning with the children. Her teachers were there to nurture the spirit as well as spark curiosity and the love of learning. They were fostering the inherent guiding force within each human being.

Partnering with and trusting this natural essence created a sense of peace within each student and thereby in the classroom community. We teachers were scientists and mystics. Learning to trust and hone our own observations and inner guidance was a key part of our mission.

In my primary classroom, I created a beautiful simple peace area where the children could go to spend time alone in silence. The sign "Peace begins with me" hung there. It was a precious place and honored by the little ones. I witnessed children learn to recognize when they felt unsettled and sought the sanctuary of that space. More importantly, I watched them discover how to find and create that calm place within themselves. Amidst our over-stimulating world, seeing this serenity in children was awe-inspiring. What would our world be like if we all had such a place and the encouragement to find our own inner peace from such a young age? I relished what I witnessed and recognized how this would serve them all as they grew to adulthood. I spent time enjoying the peaceful sanctuary as well.

Near our peace area, we also kept a silk rose. The rose was a symbol for kindness and peaceful resolution of conflict. Any time a disagreement arose between students, one would walk over, get the peace rose and bring it to their classmate. Only the child holding the rose could speak and would use phrases such as, "I felt sad when you touched my work." Back and forth the rose was passed until the clear, kind, open communication became understanding, acceptance and resolution. Here too, I witnessed daily miracles and imagined what our world would be like if we were all taught to communicate respectfully with one another in this way, even amidst our conflicts.

I envisioned adults balanced between their sense of self and their commitment to the community. I saw people who could follow their inner compasses throughout life finding direction to their natural growth and life contributions. I imagined the ability to communicate with clarity and kindness.

Most importantly, I recognized that as each person, from child to adult, was responsible for their own sense of peace and created that peace within them it truly was the start of a peaceful revolution.

Hope certainly lies within the child and that child still lives inside each of us. We can truly walk through the world radiating this sense of peace, realizing always "Peace begins with me."

DeAnne Wolfgram, Henderson
A founding former teacher at Foothills Montessori School (Henderson)
Creator & Facilitator of Conscious Connections NOW
www.deannewolfgram.com

♥

AMEN IS NOT THE END

I used to leave him standing there alone after my Amen, in the garden among the dewy roses with a heart full of the joy we shared that none other will ever know. He never waived goodbye from the other side of the locked gate. He just watched me walk back in to the world and sighed. He was always there when I returned, though, and was always happy to see me so I never thought much about his feelings.

Then one crisp spring morning he shocked me. Most of our words that morning were mine. I talked and whined from rose bush to rose bush, from the American Beauties to the blooming Marie De Blois. I complained louder than the falling waters in the fountain. I bared my soul under every vine-covered arch and on the path through the mums and chrysanthemums. By the time we got to the gate on the other side of the garden I had nothing left, except the dread of another impossible day. My emotional balloon was empty and I should have felt better, but I didn't.

That's when he said it.

"Abide with me."

"What? Abide with you??"

"Abide with me."

"I can't stay here with you. I have to go to work. People depend upon me. I have responsibilities. Listen, I absolutely adore being with you, but I have a life to live outside this garden."

I expected him to look disappointed, but he just smiled, like he expected me to "get it" at any moment. He laid a nail-scared hand on my shoulder and looked me in the eyes, and then I got it.

"Oh! You want to come with me! Well, that's a great idea, but really I don't know if you'd enjoy some of the things I have to do, and some of the people I have to work with. I live in Las Vegas and work in a casino, you know."

Again he said

"Abide with me."

I could tell there would be no arguing with him, and we were already at the gate. So I swung the thing wide and said, "Let's go then. It'll be an adventure!"

We rode the bus together, and he helped me with my work and showed me how to bless my boss and fellow workers, and even my customers. When we got home he sat with me and my family and laughed over our dinner conversations. Bedtimes were much easier, and bath times were a bit warmer with him around too. I think he was still there when I nodded off on the couch, but I had to look for him in the Garden the next day.

"Why did you go?" I asked him.

He told me how he loved abiding with me everywhere I went, and even wanted to do it again every day, but that didn't mean he wanted to give up our private place. There were things he wanted to disclose to me, private things. He wanted to tell me I was his own, and that could be a little embarrassing for me anywhere else but in The Garden. He also liked calling me, and then seeing me show up to walk and talk with him alone.

We continued walking together in The Garden every day, but it didn't end there. From then on Amen was a different word to me. It was not a period ending my prayers but an agreement and a unity that spurred on our walking and brought power to our planning, performing, and learning. Instead of locking him behind the gate the word "Amen" cut the bolt that secured the Garden door and tossed it into the bushes. It released us into a deeper, minute-by-minute), walking and talking relationship.

We still love dewy roses but now before we leave the garden we usually take a few Marie De Blois with us to share with each other and those around us throughout our day. Amen and Amen, and let's go!

DW Grant, Las Vegas
www.dwbookstore.com
Author of Blindman's Run

♥

CREATE HOPE

Within us is both good and evil. Whoever got that notion is due royalties for a whole bunch of devil and angel stickers found on trucks throughout the good ole US of A — might have been Forrest Gump!

It's hard to dismiss the notion. So called "good people" do bad things and, thankfully, "bad people" sometimes do good things. But what civilization relies on is that more good is being done than bad.

Who knows? This might be the case now. We certainly can't look to the media to persuade us of that. Unlike Forrest's box of chocolates, we can be pretty sure we're going to get many tales of human failure in our daily news.

This misrepresents reality. Whether true or not, I *choose* to define my life by *declaring* that humans are basically good. Our collective glass is more than half full.

Did you catch what I just did? I *declared* it. I *chose* to live my life on that premise, moving beyond the limbo of analysis, discouragement and fear. I also *choose* to reject pessimism and to challenge the afflicted to reconsider the efficacy of their bent.

It is neither trite nor simpleminded to *declare* that we all share a history, a tiny planet, many values, certain failings and a common fate – we are all destined to die. We must all acknowledge the rich, the poor and those in between, that the circumstances into which we are born largely define our life's paths, but not always. There is no more certainty in life from being rich than poor, being white than black, being educated than ignorant for lack of education, being beautiful or not so much. Each of us is birthed with gifts and burdens through no fault or credit of our own.

Yes, we see rich people fail and poor people rise up. But most people live comfortably within our pre-defined realm. So what do we hope for? That humanity rises up together to enjoy greater lives, liberties and happiness.

The hope for that lies here: The more we can simply accept people of all types and backgrounds and forego our tendency to judge, the more basic human goodness is revealed. The more we have compassion for those engrossed in life's challenges, the clearer we see our inescapable bonds. And with that, the greater the hope that we will all prosper together.

Kicking Pollyanna and socialism to the curb, today too many of us create enemies in our minds. "If your thoughts are not my thoughts, you are my enemy and I need to be wary of you." Too many of us are willing to destroy friendships and abandon family relations in the quest for righteousness or self-interest. Shame on us!

The decisions and choices we make shape our lives and those around us. Decide to be good, do well and see the good in others. If enough of us can do this, we hopefully change the world.

Chip Evans, Reno Nevada

♥

LOVE AND LIGHT

LIGHT, I am, amid despair
Transformative shift; now blessed & aware
LOVE, I am, amid the hate
Inspired and uplifted; with purpose I create
POWER, I am, amid the lie
Honesty grants me wings to fly
PRESENCE, I am, amid the void
Clarity of now peacefully enjoyed
TRUTH
I am that I am
And ever will be
BELIEVE
You are Love, You are Light,
You are FREE

Annabelle Husson, Las Vegas
truefreedomwithessentialoils.com

♥

IRONIC AND INSPIRATIONAL

After witnessing the suicide of my late husband, my life turned upside down. Having a gun held to my head taught me something valuable and it wasn't only how valuable my life is. It was something more important that: being congruent. On that day, I was lying unconscious for a couple of hours in our bedroom, when I woke up looking for him, upon entering the back yard I was quietly pulled out by a SWAT team. At the hospital, judging by the look on the CSI's face, I must have looked horrifying after the extensive beating. Dark haunting memories of that day stayed to torture me day and night.

My family was expecting me to move back to Hungary; hence I have no relatives in the United States.

What made me stay, I don't know. Michelle, my best friend offered me a room to stay to get away from my home until I get on my feet and I can think straight again. I ate very little and my physical and mental health was degrading. I realized very fast that antidepressant drugs pulled a haze of uncertainty on my decisions and I constantly felt sorry for myself. I got off of pills very quickly although I was advised against it.

What I choose to do was something unconventional, something strange that I knew little about. I flew to Toronto, Canada to see a master coach specialized in Neuro-Linguistic Programming (NLP) and Time Line Therapy® to get rid of my post-traumatic stress. Suki turned my life around in 6 hours. The positive effects were so profound and so fast that I stayed an extra 3 days in Toronto to prove her wrong. She sent me home on day 4 assuring me that the fear, guilt, hurt, sadness and anger will never ever haunt me again and I have to find something better to fill my days with instead of digging for past emotions.

I am a certified trainer of NLP and Time Line Therapy®. I have the best partner that I can imagine, David, in my life to support me on my plan to live a happy, content and beautiful life. The lesson that I have learned that day from my late husband is being congruent. He was an NLP trainer, just what I have become. How ironic is this situation; we both used the same technology of NLP to get what we want. He died, and I built a new life using the same tools. I proved to myself that not the skills and knowledge will form my success, but how well I know myself. My values and my personality traits are guiding me through difficult times.

I developed a passion to help people find their astonishingly unique values and their relationships to personality traits. How distinctively we weave our own fabric of reality based on who we are. Once you know what you stand for or at least you glimpsed at it, nothing that you be, do, and have can be limited by others. You become the cause of your life and you are at peace. As soon as you realize that you have stopped asking the question, What is my passion?", you have found your passion. Terramind is a business standing on the solid foundation of passion and congruency.

Anita Babinszki, Las Vegas

♥

THE WOMAN CLOTHED
WITH THE SUN

There is an image of conscious femininity, of Lady Wisdom as our modern Goddess, which speaks to most women and me about our purpose and power.

A great portent appeared in heaven: a *Woman* clothed with the sun, with the moon under her feet, and on her head a crown of twelve stars. She was pregnant, giving birth to a Savior.

This is the image of a Goddess, yet she is also a Woman. She is called Lady Wisdom. She is you and me. It is also an image we saw in July 1969 when men first landed on the Moon and sent us pictures of Earth, hanging above the Moon, surrounded by the Stars.

This heavenly *Woman* is Goddess, Earth and woman, and all three are laboring to bring new life to our people and our planet. She is clothed in the light of consciousness, for light banishes the darkness of injustice, unconsciousness and ignorance. She has her standpoint on the Moon, the regulator of earthly rhythms and tides and the eye of the Unconscious. And she is crowned with twelve Stars, which represent the twelve astrological signs that symbolize the archetypal human journey toward consciousness, wholeness and wisdom. It is a most painful and dangerous journey, yet like labor, once begun it will not stop until it has run its course. The *Woman* cries out in anguish, for the convulsions of birth are overwhelming. The child she is giving birth to wants to be born. This *Woman* is birthing something awesome and something new, otherwise the regressive energy of the patriarchy would not try to destroy her and her child, who is the awakening to our own divinity, as well as the honoring of our humanity.

This *Woman* calls all women to their purpose and destiny. It is a time for women to reclaim their ancient powers and wisdom as we deal with the anxieties of these chaotic times. These are the powers of inner sight and vision, of empathy and healing. These powers have always come from women's connection with the Earth, and as women re-discover our own spiritual power, it is not surprising that we return to an Earth-based, body-based spirituality. Feminine Spirit is the archetypal energy of the *incarnation* of Spirit. It is concerned with the *spiritualization of matter*, with the knowledge that all created things and beings partake of Spirit. We cannot afford to believe that this world is an illusion and that our true rewards lie in some heavenly paradise reserved for the elect. It is this very idea that has led us into the trouble we now find ourselves in. Our children's future is at stake.

Lady Wisdom is calling to us to walk the path of Wisdom. As women leave behind the constraints of having to live up to masculine ideas of *who we should be*, and become *who we are meant to be*, we will become Wisdom's daughters. And that will change everything.

Cathy Pagano, Las Vegas
www.wisdom-of-astrology.com
Author of *Wisdom's Daughters: How Women Can Change the World*

♥

ADOPTION DAY

"Today is not just any day;
it's more than words can say.
I dreamed and prayed for many days,
yet nothing prepares you for today.
Today is more than just a day,
10 times better than yesterday.
Today is your day, our day,
THE day, our family's Adoption Day."

Vickie Wilson, Las Vegas
Department of Family Services Adoption Recruiter

♥

HER SMILE

Is
Silent Smooth
A Mystery in a Sea Of Love
Waiting To Open Up
Unveiling Her Innermost Intimate Secret
As Questions Of Desire Float By
Her Beauty
Is
Captivating
Drawing You In
Be Careful--You May Get Lost In...
Her Eyes
Enticing Your Thoughts
To Travel Into
Her Warmth
Of
Pleasure
Her Willful Wayward Ways
Leading You To...
Her Smile
That
Simply Has a Secret

She Chooses Not To Reveal...
Just Yet

And As Attractive As She Is
You Are Impressed
By Her Smile

Vernon J Davis Jr., Las Vegas
www.vernonjdavisjr.com
Author of the *Emosewa Woman* (2nd Edition)

♥

YOGA AS A PATH TO PEACE

Yoga enjoys popularity today that teachers and students in the 1970's could only dream about. Yoga in Sanskrit means Union. I first came to Yoga as a young pregnant woman over 14 years ago trying to connect with my unborn son. Sent by my OB for relaxation I found so much more. Our teacher Kali offered a gateway to my first glimpse of real Peace, she also informed my skeptical heart that one day teaching Yoga would become my Path. She was right.

Single parenting was very challenging and relocating to the Desert from NYC was like dropping an alien into an earthquake. Knowing nobody I returned to what helped me before Yoga. My sanctuary through toddler years, marriage, another pregnancy and ultimately stage 4 Lymphoma.

Yoga shatters all illusions of who we think we are and brings us back to what is intrinsically good about ourselves; it returns us to our true nature. When we let go of a day's or week's stress we create space in the mind, body, soul and breathe for new experiences. We become free from the bondage of our past and pain; we become present. In those moments we become more open, freer and actually peaceful.

Yoga is an ancient tradition and so many styles exist in the world and in the desert of Las Vegas. I practice and teach the Satyananda style of Yoga from the Bihar School in India. We join the practice of asana (poses), pranayama (breathing control), dhyana (meditation) and samadhayo (enlightenment). The focus remains on healing from the inside out. Many of my students are seeking relief from pain or illness, and Yoga offers that lighted path to Peace.

Yoga is meditation, relaxation, movement, and breathing-a Pathway to Peace.

Namaste & Love

Heather Bruton, Las Vegas
MSW, CYT~Certified Hatha Yoga Instructor
www.omsweetomyogalv.com

♥

___

ARE YOU READY TO HEAR THE QUIET WHISPER?

___

In my twenties when I thought my life was going well, I was introduced to a teacher.

He instantly asked me about my mental chatter.

"I don't have any." I said.
He explained what chatter was, I repeated I didn't have any.
He looked at me, angrily. "Go home, boy, you're too stupid."

After two weeks of cursing mentally, suddenly, hell broke loose in my head. Reluctantly, I called the teacher and made another appointment.

At my arrival, he graciously greeted me and invited me in. I sheepishly smiled and I complained about the chatter.

"That is what you are here for, isn't?" He then explained the 'Emotional Tone Scale'. At the top is Peace where one does not hear any chatter because there is none, at the bottom is apathy where one does not hear chatter either, because it is continuous and one is not aware of the miserable life one is leading.

You are aware now. So, tell me about your chatter."
"I hear this incoherent noise, yet, I can't grasp anything."
He trained me to hear and write down the words. He told me, "Each word represents a painful incident. You must clear every one of them. When you have no mental or verbal complaints, your mind is silent, you are at peace. Then you will hear the QUIET WHISPER."

Several years later I still had frequent chatter. Then I met a teacher which I promptly told how smart I was. "However", I said, "I can't do your training because I am broke." He answered, " Yes, I am very expensive, yet, I would like very much to work with you and you being as smart as you say you are, could do a project for me and I would gladly work with you for free."

I immediately accepted the offer.

He introduced me to five geometrical shapes called Tatwas. "They are from ancient India." He explained, "They are powerful energies. You combine these five Tatwas with each other and tell me what each of the twenty five combinations represents."
"Is this all you want?" I asked.
"Yes."

On the way home I discovered two combinations which

128

made me believe I could complete the project within days!

However it took eighteen years of many hours a day to complete the task. I had become very fascinated by the Tatwas. I had developed a way to meditate on each combination with great result. Yet, my major discovery was that they greatly quieted down my chatter by releasing painful incidents!

I created a combination a few years into the project, which I called 'Key Zero'. My meditation it took me into a dark cave with a dim light in the distance. The moment I thought of going to the light, I was floating in light outside of the cave freely in total peace.
I don't know why I suddenly said, "Greetings Father."
A warm, quiet voice whispered, "Greetings my son."

Emahmn, Las Vegas
www.magicmandala.com
Author of *Book of Correspondences*

♥

___

THE ENERGY OF PEACE

___

A Message from a Newborn

Being a few weeks old, newly born into this family and hearing you talk about how everything operates on earth, I have a burning question.

Are you saying that humans have not figured out Peace yet?
That is most incredible, because it's so easy! It's in fact the easiest thing on earth and elsewhere. Ah, you did not know?
Well, ok, here is what you do.
You have to start understanding the innate programming of children.

You see, we are programmed with two main features:

1. Freedom of Movement.
2. Play, Play and Play.

We, children have to develop our bodies; discover our unique self, how to live on the planet, and how to relate to other beings. We resolve our conflicts, we trade, and we show how we care for each other. We imitate, find out what we like, we take turns in leading, we match our energies.

Have you ever watched a flock of birds dancing in the sky or a school of fish swirl through the water? That is the cooperative energy that any group of beings can create.

The other day when you introduced me to some parents on the playground, I saw a few kids creating this. They were standing together and all of a sudden they ran off, to one side, and then again together to the other side.

This cooperative energy can develop into The Energy of Peace. You must understand how necessary it is that a child can be a child. When we have the freedom of movement and play, we grow into individuals with unique selves, caring, providing and serving in all aspects of life. That is all! Can you see how easy it is?

However, if you do not understand and trust that we require the unlimited freedom of movement and play, you might only see children acting foolishly with other children. You consider it as wasting our time and you may get scared. You feel you must 'prepare' us for a harsh adult world. You become the boss and owner of us. This disturbs our innate child programming. We learn how to boss other children and even boss you and other adults. If we were disturbed in our programming we still use the cooperative energy, but we flock with those who are also disturbed and we may form gangs.

To establish The Energy of Peace, you have to consciously re-learn what was disturbed in your own life, healing wounds of not being trusted as a child yourself. Meanwhile, you have to allow us to do our innate child programming and become providing, caring, serving adults with a unique self.

You see, we have these little bodies, and we want to play all the time, but that does not mean that we do not see what is going on.

Cielja Kieft, Las Vegas
www.PositiveParentingAFreeChild.com
Author of *Grateful for My New Baby*

♥

EMPOWERING WOMEN
BEGINS IN YOUTH

As the mother of three sons who have become loving, caring, and compassionate men I want to share a bit of inspiration. There were two statements that I often shared with my sons, throughout life. The first one being, "There are no mistakes in life, only lessons". As Albert Einstein said, "Learn from yesterday, live for today, hope for tomorrow".

When my sons wanted something that I could not afford or could not get for them, I was honest with them as I said, "There will always be those that have more than you, AND there will always be those with less. A mother who does not oblige in her son's every request is building a relationship with her son that teaches them acceptance and strength that will last a lifetime. A father can teach his son a great deal by being a good role model. However, Mothers, your bond with your son is one like no other. They look up to you, they watch you closely. They want your approval. Mothers play a crucial role in how their sons interact and view women. Show your son the same respect that you want them to honor you with.

Many men are uncomfortable simply listening to someone sharing with emotion. They are often times thinking of how they can fix things. Men, when a woman is sharing something emotional with you the number one thing that they wish for is that they are heard. By being capable of repeating what is being said is what a woman often needs. To know that the words they are speaking are being heard is a comforting and satisfying gift. Teach your sons to respect and view women as the great contributors to society that they are. Teach them to listen. Teach your sons how to empower women. Start when they are boys. Although it is never too late as a son values the words of wisdom from his mother, even if they do not admit it. Men recognize the strength of women. Just as you can acknowledge how they contribute to the family, know that they are capable of so much more. Society needs strong women and the world is full of them. Acknowledge women for all that they accomplish and the world will flow with love.

Love can dissolve so many negative energies. Allow the women of the world to do what comes naturally.

So you see, it is mutual respect for one another that will create a better world. Re-write the old messages that run through your mind regarding the division of the sexes. Do not look at life the same anymore. Do what feels good in your heart. Love one another like you have never done before. We can all shower each other with an abundance of love. We all want the same outcome when it comes to living our daily lives. We all wish to be able to be our true self and experience love and respect while doing so.

Jill Bachhuber, Las Vegas

♥

LAUGHTER MAKES EVEN THE DARKER DAYS BRIGHTER

My mother always told my sister and I that smiles and laughter will help make even the darkest things easier to deal with. That was her wise philosophy and the way she lived her life for nearly 97 years. It was my pleasure to edit her memoir, *Can We Come In and Laugh, Too?*, when she was 80 years old.

I have always looked for the humor, and so did my sister, Phyllice Bradner. We use it generously in our Silver Sisters Mysteries, a funny crime caper series. Not only that, but when we've had to face some tough situations, laughter got us through and helped us keep our faith that everything would work out.

Last year the power of humor and laughter was really driven home when I was diagnosed with early stage breast cancer. All during the surgery, chemotherapy and radiation I tried to find something funny in the situation and so did my sister who was very supportive. Like when all of my hair fell out and she said, "Well, on the plus side, you'll finally find out what color your hair really is when it grows back."

I got three wigs: short platinum, short auburn and long auburn. I had fun with the folks at the radiation facility and oncologist's office by showing up in a different wig each time. They began to take bets about which Morgan I would be.

The message about laughter being healing couldn't have been clearer, because I recovered rapidly, and didn't spend any time feeling sorry for myself. When I had after-effects from the chemo, I gave into them, flaked out for a few days and then enjoyed the time until the next treatment. Fortunately, there were only four.

When I got my walking papers from the radiation oncologist, incidentally 7 treatments before the total number, he originally thought I would need, he said he was sure my sunny attitude speeded my recovery. Everyone at that facility told me how much my smiles and jokes would be missed and how they wished more patients were able to have that kind of outlook.

I'm back to my old Energizer Bunny-self now, still looking at the bright side every day. During the time I was under treatment I'd even worked on two books. One, *La Bella Mafia*, the true story of Bella Capo, co-authored by Dennis Griffin and me, will be released around October 2013. It is a tale of abuse, survival and giving back, not for the faint-of-heart and guess what Bella credits her survival to in part—laughter and finding the humor in the worst situations. Years ago I heard Norman Cousins speak about how he beat cancer and guess what? He also credited a large portion of his recovery to humor and laughter.

Paste a smile on your face, look for the humor in even the worst situations, and don't waste time feeling sorry for yourself. Trust me—it really helps. I know from years of experience.

Morgan St. James, Las Vegas
www.morganstjames-author.com
Author of *La Bella Mafia*, the shocking true story of Bella Capo

♥

HELP YOURSELF AND OTHERS OVERCOME NEGATIVITY

Once while meditating I pleaded with the heavenly hosts to help me deal with a woman who had twice tried to get me fired from my job. I dreaded seeing her that day at a meeting and needed divine guidance.

The message I received was stunningly simple. *Send her God's love.*

So right before I faced her expected volcano of negativity, I found a quiet spot where I could be alone. I prayed to the Great I Am to fill me with heavenly light and love to such a degree that it would saturate every cell of my being. I asked to be used as a conduit to send this most precious of all gifts to her.

I strolled into the classroom where our meeting was to take place. With sweating palms and a lurching stomach, I silently asked the Most Supreme Being to help me release my nervousness and to continue to fill me with love and positivity.

I found my seat and took a deep breath to center myself. When she strolled in, I sent waves of godly affection to her.

Her reaction was immediate. She cast an odd look my way. Plus, I detected a hint of surprise on her face.

I smiled, finding I could relax and stay out of my defensive mode.

Oh, Highest of Powers, keep it coming. It's working!

She returned the grin. And when she spoke, her usual cynical tone softened. God's love neutralized her insecurity, anger and adversarial demeanor.

After that experience, I make it a habit to send divine adoration whenever I feel nervous about encountering someone I perceive as hostile. And, you know what? It's worked every time, except when I start to doubt the divine or refused to relinquish my own negativity toward that person.

3 steps to overcoming another's negativity

Through radiating love we can make the world better for all of us.

1. Instead of absorbing peoples' hostilities, we can recognize them and offer them up to the Most Supreme Being.

2. We can will ourselves to serve as vessels filled with love and projecting divine love. Let's smile and resist the temptation to become antagonized.

3. Pray for strength and to see these individuals as godly creations.

We gain nothing by returning harmful energies and we dishonor ourselves by internalizing them. We don't have to love these people, but we can gift them with this most positive of emotions.

Through divine intervention, we can break the cycle of hatred and help heal the world one person at a time. God's love handles it all.

Kathleen Berry, Sparks Nevada
www.kathleenberry.com
Author of *A Reluctant Spirit: A True Tale of God, Ghosts and a Skeptical Christian*

♥

SPIRIT

You've taken many painful lumps
Survived life's tearful turns
Endured some brutal bruises, bumps,
And saintly savage burns

Be grateful for the strength you've gained
Your inner muscles bulge
But lips are drained and legs are chained
By fears you still indulge

Your animator kept from view
Locked up inside a cell
It pleads release long overdue
While you secure the shell

If you should seek to sow the seed
Of peace within your heart,
The breathless breather must be freed
No secret self apart

Your essence never lacks the nerve
It's power shines divine
To be in spirit is to serve

With courage by design

So dig your cowardice a grave
And lower it to rest
Your daring, dauntless dreams will save
The slave still dispossessed

Steve Pavlina, Las Vegas

www.stevepavlina.com

Author of Personal Development for Smart People-Accelerate Your Growth

♥

BECCA'S STORY

February 8th, 1989 came as a usual day and yet I had a strong sensation of fear-*more than I can ever remember in my life*. I intuitively knew I was seriously ill. *I was about to walk into my appointment with Dr. Christensen and the gut wrenching fear was gripping me.*

A few days before, on February the 5th, I awoke around 5am. As I lay in bed, I began to meditate and a message came in from the Angels, Universe-God and it frightened me. The message was an answer to a question I had asked during meditation. *It was two words: Lymphoma Cancer.* I heard this as if someone was standing *right* in front of me. I came out of this state thinking: "What the hell is Lymphoma?"

I began to pray like never before. I requested speediness in the diagnosis and *for the Universe to align me with all the doctors I would need. I had heard stories of people getting sent from one doctor to another and I knew that I did not have time.* In fact, I was running out of time in a way that I hadn't even grasped.

After walking into my appointment *I found myself sit-*

ting in the paper clothing they give you for examinations. I waited... I prayed... and I envisioned white, green and violet light running through me-beginning at the top of my head and racing through my entire body. To me, this was God and his energy rushing through me. Dr. Christensen walked in, introduced himself and immediately began to examine my neck. By then, the bulging lumps looked like an ugly mass of knots, each one about the size of a quarter. Dr. Christensen performed his exam and proceeded to ask for the name of my family physician, Dr. Miller, to discuss my diagnosis. When he hung up the phone, he turned to me with a tear in his eye and said: "Dear, I am afraid you have **Lymphoma Cancer.**"

I was immediately sent upstairs to an oncologist, Dr. Kingsley who *began the process of blood drawings and extensive exams.* A couple of days later, I had day surgery to do the biopsies including a bone marrow biopsy. A few days later, I was told I had Non-Hodgkin's Lymphoma Cancer, stage 4 of 4 and it was in my bone marrow.
A nurse stated I had about 30 days to live.

That was 24 years ago and I am healthy, strong and disease free. I believe by the power of prayer, meditation, visualization and faith I was able to move forward into the future.

Rebecca Fountain, Las Vegas
Native Nevadan since 1961
Rebecca@SpiritualTheory.com

♥

THE RIPPLE EFFECT

I marveled at the calmness &
the placidness of this pool....
Then, a pebble amidst the still waters plunged...
A hollow sound...
Then silence
The circling waves rippled on and on and on
...in a moment they were gone
And the calmness of the pool was again within my view
Oh, but how the tempest rages!
...for however mild the swell or slight the flood
The placidity of this lough is disturbed &
its bottom waters are no more still...
You are the pebble in this: my pool
for you touched the deep well of my heart
bringing within me a rise
flowing as not to cease...
But, in a moment,
you, like the ripples of the pool appeared to be gone
& the undulation surrounding me
seemed to calm and still as though at peace
Oh, but how my heart billowed!!
For, no matter the gentleness of the plunge
or slight the swell

you disturbed my innermost being....&
now, I revamp my depths...
...Calm my rapids
that you may see the peace on my surface waters
...Not the splashing waves abyss
for, like the placid pool,
I am still no more

It is said that people come into our lives for a season; a reason; a lifetime.

I disagree. Once someone has entered your life, the impact is permanent. They never go. There is an indelible imprint at the very core of your being. Besides, why would you want them to leave? When someone or something has influenced to the core, there is a "ripple effect"....a gradual spreading of change or influence.

A gradually spreading effect or influence.

Have you ever planted a seed and waited for it to grow? Well, let's think about. Once the seed is planted the soil is forever changed. The nutrients, the water the displacing of the soil...changed forever. From that one seed grows a harvest greater than itself. It is not an overnight transformation; it happens gradually, slowly and consistently. So, looking at the ripple effect, the pebble in the pool if you would, you see the initial impact, then you see the calm and stillness of the pool. The pool is never the same because of the impact of the small change that took place in the glint of a moment.

How changed are you because someone took the time to smile or compliment you or touch your hand? What small impression, impact, or imprint has moved you to change or shift your focus or view? Remember the unexplained smile, the uncharacteristic gleam in your eyes, the warm glow that engulfs your spirit? We can never know when that "something" is going to be the catalyst to propel us to our greatness. However, when life happens, be ready and willing to flow with it.

Jamillah Ali Rashada, Las Vegas

♥

HE WOKE ME UP

He woke me up this morning
I did not hear a loud sound, nor see an image, nor feel a
touch
He woke me up this morning
My eyes opened up and I sat up in bed with a feeling of
joy
He woke me up this morning
My body felt like a smile on a child's face, after seeing a
new puppy
He woke me up this morning
The joy was so uplifting that words could not describe it
He woke me up this morning
My mind was alert and my heart was receptive
He woke me up this morning
In no pain, saw no anger, felt no sorrow
He woke me up this morning
Like a, fresh morning dew, I felt blessed to witness
Thank you for the blessing
Jesus...

Monica Johnson-Williams, Las Vegas
www.bacclv.org
Author of *A Hero is a Man who tried his best*

♥

SENDING LIGHT

Sending Love, Light and Prayers in every Universal and Cosmic Direction, Dimension and Plane.

Reflections

We are all reflections of God, Spirit, Source, and Light,
We are reflections of One another,
Choose to be reflections of Love, Peace and Harmony,
We are One Love,
Pure Love is Not an Illusion.

Grateful

I AM grateful for the many friends, family and blessings in my life, and for the awareness of unity, love and light within each of us, we are one.

One Message

Love, Love, Love, Love, Love, Love, Love....Nuff said :)

Be the Light

My father taught me that laughter is healing and that real men cry, and to care, love and respect deeply.

I danced on his feet, put ribbons in his hair, and painted his nails.

He taught me that compassion is a must and dignity is a plus.

He taught me to be myself and that was more than

enough.

He taught me to dance like no one is watching, and to smile more than once in a while.

He taught me that the world can be cruel but humor would rule, and that a hug would make everything right.

He taught to pray and to give all problems to God so that he would lead the way.

He taught me that when things are dark...to turn on the light.

Heal Thyself

Dance in the rain,

Cleanse your soul,

Your heart,

Your pain,

Dance in the rain.

Imelda Perez McCarthy, Las Vegas

♥

LITANY AND CHANT

Rain fell last night;
now worms that found no dry places to bury themselves
lie floating on the grass; trees dropped pounds of water
onto the wind, into the ground, down to the pond;
there frogs wake under heavy leaves and watch bubbles
leap through slimed water and break into breeze.

I am green, I am budding, my eyes look for the sun.
Dog wanders these dank fields
water's made musky-alive;
another dropped this mound
and pissed to tell this dog some news,
but rain's washed most of that
smell-speech to the stream.

I am swollen, I am limpid, my tongue hungers for stones.
Sparrow tastes this morning's grain,
sees exhausted worms gasping in the grass,
shakes dampness from her wings;
so quick now, her dive down
such dewy air to feed...

I am empty, I am falling, I seek root in earth.
Mist-spectacled, naked man squints at dawn
over trees; wet grass slivers curl on his toes;
his neck trembles, hair on his skin alerts;
his mouth opens, teeth ache in chilled air,
he spreads his arms and his heart
touches the Sun's...

I am empty, I am swollen, I am liquid, I am stone;
I am rooted, I am wind, I am falling;
Rains leaped in my ears, tears drenched my eyes;
now I offer my weight wholly to the Sun.
Green I am and loam I am, gold I am and wing I am;
blood I am and tree I am, mouth I am and ear I am;
stalk I am and fire I am, rain I am and claw I am;
tooth I am and cry I am; grave I am O sea I am;
leap I am O Sun I am;
I am, I am, I am...

Nicholas Marco, Las Vegas

♥

THE RIGHT FLOW OF INTUITION

Slow down, breathe, and listen for the inner voice,
Angel advice, your intuition.
Ask to receive divine preparation,
To hear without static, guiding words
For the greater good.

When the answer is right,
You will find the path of least resistance.
It will harm no thing
For it comes from a place of love.

Then release yourself from ego.
You feel neither conflict nor competition,
Knowing there is plenty for all
In the eternal distinctiveness of Universal abundance.

Pieces float together seamlessly.
You encounter serendipitous connections.
Everything works as smoothly as it should.
Questions you pondered are answered.

Close your eyes, sense the sway of timeless current
As if being gently rocked in the arms of a loving parent.
It feels good to you because it is good for all.
It is the right flow of intuition

Adrianne Carlino Gentile, Las Vegas, Nevada
Author of 66 *LEAVES Poems From My Tree of Life*

♥

HOPE

There are many people who unfortunately have some kind of Mental Disorder such as Bi-Polar (manic depressive illness) and are not aware of it or don't know how to control it. Many go unnoticed and are thought of as passive/aggressive or worst yet, temperamental.

There is a stigma tied to being manic depressive. People don't see your mental disorder as a real illness. "It's all in your head. Get over it." These powerful sentences are the most hurtful of all. We victims do not have control over how our brain's chemical imbalance makes us feel or not feel.

It's no different than if our liver was not making enough insulin to metabolize sugar. In theory it's no different, but in perception it's very different. People accept a diabetic but won't tolerate a mentally ill person.

When I talk about Hope, I mean that there is help out there.

Many victims and their families today are more understanding and patient when mental illness is identified. They learn how to deal with it and move forward. Once that happens life is full of delight and peace, and there's an increase in the acceptance of the mentally ill. Acceptance — this one word gives me hope for my future. It gives me hope for yours, too.

My peace comes from my family. When I first learned I was Bi-polar and how the illness affected me, I told my family and friends about it. Once I educated them, and they researched it on their own, my life and theirs became filled with peace, love and harmony.

It has not been an easy journey; there are still times in my life when my illness makes me want to end it. However, my family is there and they take the necessary steps to help me move on.

Sometimes, I try to go outside and take a deep breath. I walk around the house or maybe around the block. When I'm done I call someone -- it doesn't matter who. I just want to hear about someone's day, and they ask me how I'm doing.

I take advantage of that and I pour out my fears to them. When I end the call, I wipe away my tears, take a deep breath and continue on. I am no longer alone.

Hope is what I have for my future and I cannot do it without my family. Hope is what I wish everyone would have to make themselves better.

If you have a mental illness, tell your friends and family. Get their help and support. With that, there's hope for you, too.

Andres Fragoso, Jr., Las Vegas
www.andresfragosojr.com
Author of Writer's Sidekick Notebooks
www.WritersSidekick.com

♥

IT SOUNDED IMPOSSIBLE

So many people who have lost loved ones from every type of tragedy imaginable are suffering in ways that most cannot begin to imagine. If the afterlife was understood as the greatest of all vacations in the most magical place instead of the dreaded graveyard filled with the scary unknown, our grief and fear could be processed and life could be more fully lived. If we could only know that the loss of a physical body is just a graduation to a more gentle and loving existence and that death cannot separate us from those we love, we could live life with a New View of life and death. Sadness and fear could be replaced with a joyful anticipation of the day we reunite with our soul family that watches us so closely. They are so close in another dimension which we have lost the memory of and cannot scientifically prove. This is one of the great mysteries, like gravity, quantum physics and creation, but it is likely the most amazing mystery of all.

Old age might even be welcomed as a preparation for the grand event filled with reflection instead of a time of severe loneliness and depression so rampant in our current society. Assume a new position regarding what some call the afterlife. Try a "New View" from the top of the world and see how much lighter your life can be. It doesn't cost anything, so give it a whirl. I did!!

It wasn't long after my son John passed, that he began communication with me clearly through the thoughts I would have. It turned out, as awful as it was to live after burying my son. It was a gift to me to work together with him on a music project after he left his physical body.
As I have no musical talent whatsoever, this idea seemed ridiculous to me so I tried very hard to ignore his constant pressure to forge on. I assure you, this pressure from him was not easy to ignore and the task he wanted me to undertake was more than difficult and required a great deal of faith and hard work on my part. I am not particularly energetic or educated. I have no background in science, technology or music. He wanted me to produce very specific music with healing frequencies and low tones, called Vibroacoustics on DVDs that would make it very easy for people to heal themselves. It sounded impossible but I did it. These gifts and special frequencies recently saved my husband's life.

This required learning, testing, reading, researching and opening my own recording studio. He presented me with everything I needed seemingly out of thin air, the people, the money, the information, the partners and the mentors as the need for each arose.

Educating people not to "Pop a pill" but instead to "Pop

in a DVD" is a difficult task – but not impossible. Neither is opening up to a new view of leaving behind the physical body.

Regina Rose Murphy, Las Vegas
Author of *The Elusive Gift of Tragedy*
emotionalsoundtechniques.com

♥

AGING AS A PORTAL OF HOPE

Aging is enriching for me. It is not to be feared or whined about. Old age is not a curse.

I just entered my 64th year of life and yes, some physical frailties are presenting themselves. I have to pee more often than I used to. I have little skin eruptions on my face, and I'm getting age spots on my hands. I take meds for an enlarged prostate, and I am borderline diabetic. Sometimes, as songwriter Leonard Cohen put it, "I ache in the places where I used to play."

However, I'm honestly enjoying my "advanced age" of 63. My optometrist said I need new lenses because my vision has *improved* in the last two years. I have a nine-month-old grandson named Micah whose smile lights me up. I have a new job in community education that gives me joy and challenge and a solid sense of self-worth. I've let go of many outdated friendships and renewed a few important ones that had slipped away.

I keep learning about human beings and computers and the diversity of life on earth and the unfathomable reaches of the cosmos. And when I've pondered that a while, I come across something like this, from Diane Ackerman's book , *An Alchemy of Mind*, "Impossible as it sounds, we have more brain cell connections than there are stars in the [visible] universe...In a dot of brain no larger than a single grain of sand, 100,000 neurons go about their work at a billion synapses. In the cerebral cortex alone, 30 billion neurons meet at 60 trillion synapses a billionth of an inch wide." No wonder I sometimes forget why I walked into a room.

I help facilitate a non-religious (but decidedly spiritual) program called the Alternatives to Violence Project in Northern Nevada prisons. Every three-day, 21-hour workshop brings me face-to-face with 20-plus inmates who are dedicated to changing the behavior that led to their incarceration. After I've heard their stories and shared my own, I leave with a heightened appreciation of human dignity, wisdom and potential for change. And I miss those guys.

"Old age is not a defeat but a victory, not a punishment but a privilege," said Jewish theologian Abraham Heschel. "One ought to enter old age as one enters the senior year at a university, in exciting anticipation of consummation."

Maybe I'm just more aware of life now. But I've come to believe, as a wise person said, that miracles are commonplace and the commonplace is a miracle. And that aging is hopeful.

Rick Sorensen, Sparks Nevada

♥

BE STILL

2013 began painfully, not that the previous 3 years were a vacation, what with my mother's death, my brother's paralysis from Prostate Cancer, and the recession—life was far from pleasant in 2010. And in January of this year life happened again, negatively impacting family, work, and my health. 'Overwhelmed' is an understatement! I've felt beaten up, nearly beaten down.

I was acutely aware of my increased stress level. So much so, that I accepted it as my companion. Even the heaviness of stress was comforting as the new familiar, like a jacket on a nippy night. Even with the weight of knowing that I was not myself, out of phase with who I am, the load was comforting in its constancy—I knew it would be there later, tomorrow, next week.

Thankfully I reached the point of being tired of hearing my patented response. When asked *"How are you?"* the standard answer had become a dismal *"I'm ok."* Something within said "this isn't ok."

My subconscious beckoned me to awaken and resist

this flatness, spiral to the abyss. *Life happens, deal with it!*

Ok. Ok. Slowly I recognized that I needed to improve my coping mechanisms. Struggling through the day because I didn't sleep well and my mind bouncing off the wall wasn't working. This sub-par me wasn't fair to my clients, patients, family, friends, or myself. I needed to cope better with my current reality. Something had to give. But what? No clue. The answer laid, I suddenly realized, in stillness. Quiet the body. Quiet the mind. My Truth will reveal itself. **Be still.**

Stillness is not laziness nor weakness nor passivity. Stillness is actively opening to the possible. Stillness is minimizing external and internal distractions to allow that wise inner voice to be heard.

Learning how to be still, to really be still and let life happen - that stillness becomes radiance. Morgan Freeman

Activity conquers cold but stillness conquers heat. Lao Tzu
I got it! Stillness for me included yoga, quiet time, rest, and reflection. But my first act of stillness was massage. I booked an appointment with my Massage Therapist and reached a level of stillness and quiet that I missed desperately.

As I settled onto the massage table, an indescribable calm enveloped me. It had been far too long since I experienced that level of inner peace. Life stress—worry, anxiety, pain stopped at the door. And although life stress continued after my massage, the worry, anxiety and pain were joined by resilience. I felt stronger, better able to cope. I was clear that the burden could be lifted. The effect of the massage was so immediate that my dismal response changed. So the next time someone asked *"How are you?"* I paused then said, *"I'm on the road to restore balance."*

Being still works. Note to self…. A great way to Be Still is through massage.

Glen Alex, Las Vegas
www.massageadvantagelv.com

♥

LOST IN LAS VEGAS?

Are you still trying to find your way and just looking for your happy place? Is life not turning out the way you planned? Well accept the obvious and go for the alternative. Don't sweat the small stuff. I know it can be overwhelming but it does all start out as small stuff. Our thoughts, energy, and the more time we put into it, the bigger it gets. We all need to take time to relax and breathe. Allow yourself to feel joy and peace. Quiet your mind and say to yourself: this too shall pass, it will all be ok. Pain happens, so does feelings of loss and despair. But ask yourself how long are you going to remain there? Because time really does go by so fast. Don't lose a minute of it on regret. You don't want to miss the beauty and opportunities presented to you. Each day come up with three things you are grateful for. Just remember that love is the most powerful thing there is. Trust me, you have more of it than you know and the more you give love, the more you will receive love. Love is service. So give whenever, wherever you can. Sometimes the best thing you can give someone is your time. So smile, laugh, cry, complain and then let it go and smile again. Because you are here for a reason and you do matter.

Sincerely,

Boni Stewart, Las Vegas

♥

A HUMAN EXPERIENCE OF SURVIVAL-AN INSPIRED ACTION OF LOVE

Throughout my life I have endured great tragedy that has lead me through a time tunnel and a passage to learn from the experience to have and not have courage, wisdom and kindness. As a child I prayed in search of happiness and the meaning of life. There are so many avenues I could have travelled to share with you my inspiration. In the beginning it wasn't easy to know what premise to focus on. Eventually, the answer was the most simple.

Life is simple. It is "A Human Experience of Survival," that is most difficult. Our greatest challenge in life is facing our fears, the acceptance of change and the battle to win and succeed that holds us captive -- it equally holds the key. During the fight to endure a survivor becomes a warrior, the battle begins and the struggle continues. It is in the surrender that we align ourselves with the freedom to discover inner peace, happiness and unconditional love.

Deborah Berry, Las Vegas
Author of *Empower Your Life, Secrets from a Life Coach*
DeborahBerry.com

♥

SHE'S SETTLING IN

She's settling in…

She's settling into those depths within herself. Those long untapped natural resources are flowing through her veins, pumping her heart and enlivening her being. She's settling into an awareness of her own humble magnificence. She's in… She's in body and embodying it. She's settling down. She's settling down into those depths and honoring the truth of who she is. "Those years filled with insecurity and anxiety are no more."

No more does she need to prove who she is to anyone, even to herself. Settling into the depths of her being, she has discovered a being that is deeply sacred, naturally beautiful, expansive and gifted. This being she is….. is multifaceted, intuitively knowing, and truly wise, immensely loving and yet…simply indescribable. She no longer needs to give herself labels or be acknowledged by the busy noisy world outside. The feeling… this knowing she has now…. is enough. She is enough. Down in her own depths she is settled. She's not settling for anything less.

She's not settling for anything less, not anymore… She knows her worth now and she will not settle for anything less than what honors her gifts and values her essence. Her presence is both powerful and empowering. She will not settle for anything less in herself either. She must hold her own now. Those others who have not done their own deep work will not be able to impact her soul anymore. She can witness them with compassion now and hold her own energy within, so they do not drain her being or suck dry her own aliveness. She will not settle for being called "less than" anymore. She knows her truth. She knows she is a vehicle for the divine on earth. Her own womb mirrors the womb of all creation. She is powerful beyond what she ever knew before this realization and yet she will never use this power to control, manipulate or wound as she has witnessed in the world. She is empowered through the creative, collaborative energy of love. She's allowing that magnificent loving power to guide her, for it to settle into every pore of her skin and atom of her body and pour out into the world through her every thought, every touch, every word, every action and every moment of simply being who she is.

She is settled now. She has settled into her own being. She knows who she is. "She is us…. now."

DeAnne Wolfgram, Henderson
www.deannewolfgram.com

♥

OPERATION POSSIBILITY

I have developed a new found love for Mercury Retrograde. Somehow it feels like I even look forward to it like it's a festival or something. I love this time of the year!

In this cocoon for 3 weeks:

Re-Evaluating (what's really important)

Re-Grouping (from being scattered in a million directions)

Re-Considering (my approach to life and how I choose to live it)

Re-Charging (the energy that I feel has been depleted)

Re-Connecting (to my spirit and inner-most desires)

Re-Mapping (the direction to the places I want to go in my life)

Re-Defining (who I am in this next stage in life)

Re-Kindling (love I have for myself & nurturing who I'm becoming)

Re-Newing (exploring different elements of myself in new ways)

And let's not forget, diving deeper into "OPERATION

POSSIBILITY"!

Inhaling great expectations and exhaling satisfaction for the next 3 weeks.

Marquetta Goodwin, Las Vegas

♥

BECAUSE I WANT TO,
THAT'S WHY

One of the easiest things for me to do is to sit down and write.

One of the hardest things for me to do...is to sit down and write.

Blame it on the A.D.D.? Partially. Or maybe blame it on my 2007 Dell Laptop that I clearly need to replace. It freezes constantly. I have wires exposed. I have considered selling my Louis Vuitton I won to buy another one. It's on my list of things to buy that falls below other things I need to pay for. And hey, I'm trying to save. But I digress.

Blaming doesn't accomplish anything. It is a time waster and a dream thief. You don't need to find reasons to NOT do things. There are a million reasons why you should and why you shouldn't. You only need ONE reason to...because YOU WANT TO. My greatest struggle with writing isn't my desire to; it is my insecurity with what I produce. If it isn't flowing perfectly from the start, I don't want to finish it. I hit a speed bump in the first 20 minutes and I give up and "toss" my words into the trash. I don't want to push through and post and have anyone read it and think "wow, she really needs to find another hobby." So it goes somewhere in the great beyond, where incomplete works, 'given-up' hopes and dreams reside. It's a bad habit I desperately want to break. So, this is me breaking it. The only way to break a habit is forming a new one. For this goal of mine (to be a writer, later motivational speaker, and save the world) it means to write more, it means putting the writing that I both loathe and love out. Otherwise this year will be a repeat of the last many. I have sat around and started countless stories, articles, and pages, some of which I had hoped would magically turn into a book. Years later, none of the unfinished works magically turned into a final piece. I didn't wake up one morning with a call from the New York Times, asking to publish a piece of my work. I didn't wake up to a book deal from a major publishing house. I didn't wake up to my dreams unfolding before my eyes. I woke up with frustration. I woke up annoyed at myself. I woke up tired of promising myself that tomorrow would be the day that I would try harder. So as I have been in other areas of my life, I'm changing course. If you want something to change, you HAVE TO DO SOMETHING. It is pro-activity that leads to progress. It is the daily grind. It isn't fairies and unicorns and glitter falling from the sky. Well, actually... I live in Vegas. However, I wake up and put my two feet down just the same as anyone else. I just have to pull off the confetti sometimes.

PREACHING TO THE CHOIR: What if YOU DON'T LOVE YOUR RESULTS? I don't most of the time. But I am unfulfilled with sitting still, and you should be too. It is practice. Creative practice. Music practice. Exercise practice. Cooking practice. Dream sharing practice. Speech practice. Whatever it is, learn to push through the process. It will eventually produce results. You might have to change course a dozen times, but how will you ever change course if you never start? Or if you keep starting and don't push yourself? If you learn to finish it out, even if you are pulling burnt cookies out of the oven 10 times, you will eventually get better, or lose your passion for it and move on. If you start playing that guitar collecting dust in your room, you will eventually start to play better, or figure out it was a waste of time and find something you DO love to do. Your ideas may not be great when you share them. Your 'talents' may not come naturally. Most of the time they will suck. And may suck bad for awhile. And that is okay. Because eventually your work(s) will start to suck less. It is progress in doing something you want to do. Fall in love with DOING. That is my biggest push right now for my OCD/ADD mind. People say "go out and try-fight for your dreams!" with passion in their voice. But I don't always feel passionate and inspired, and on those days it is just as important to go through the motions. Create habits in your creativity and talents to finish it out to the end. Share your ideas. Good or bad. Play the guitar. Good or bad. Cook. Good or bad. "Just Do it!"

So I started writing today, as I do many times, and it is a mess of thoughts. A wreck of ideas. A disaster of quality. And that makes it perfect. Because I completed it. I am loving my dreams/talents/goals in the 'good and the bad'. For better or for worse. We can't grow without the grind. Peace, love and coffee

Char Modelle, Las Vegas

♥

WATCHING FROM AFAR

In the fall of 2011 I was privileged to receive a scholarship to attend Stanford School of Medicine for a conference on social media and patient care. There is something about walking in the rarified company of lauded researchers from Stanford, Harvard, Pew, NIH and Mayo Clinic and bear witness to their humble brilliance. Despite this surreal experience, the moments engraved on my heart had nothing to do with academics, but people. Not just any people, real people, flesh and blood patients from all walks of life. These are individuals who struggle daily, some with rare diseases, others fighting battle after battle with cancer coupled with trying to live "normally." Social media has become a conduit for support and information. All of us are patients at some point in our lives; it's just that the specter of sickness is usually slain. Not everyone is as lucky. So in the spirit of life's real warriors, many I've been privileged to meet, I dedicate this story.

* * *

I wasn't invited to the party, but I frequently look in on the arrangement of remarkable females with awe, much like that of a 13 year-old girl surreptitiously observing her older sister and her best friends discussing adult topics like wardrobes and sex.

The women in this group are no longer in their teens though many wistfully remark on the passage of time since being young college students, fledgling mothers or in the throes of their first love affair to where they are now. All of these women are indeed grown-up even if some of them are only in their twenties. And not just because of chronology, because of experience.

They meet regularly. So I peer on them regularly. I'm silent because I don't want my attendance to be noticed. Does that make me a voyeur? Not that I think I'd be unwelcome but because it's a group I'm afraid of joining and yet I know that I could unwittingly become a member. Ironically this group does not recruit.

I am fascinated by these women.

While their meetings do not occur in lecture halls or even in quaint tea rooms, they exude the same academic power and congeniality if only in the virtual space they occupy. In this group, each woman has their own room in which they often retreat to collect their thoughts and wage an intimate battle that we as observers or even as other members cannot fully appreciate. Some immerse themselves in complex scientific discussions, others bake cookies, and all support each other.

I watch from afar.

Today's meeting was different though and I found out about it incidentally. @whymommy and @ccchronicles were trending on Twitter. The blogosphere was atwitter. And the rooms reserved for these respective members— ToddlerPlanet and CancerCultureNow—were decidedly dark.

With greater speed than Paul Revere, but one equally urgent, it was announced that members Rachel Cheetham Moro and Susan Niebur, one a Brown University alumni with a beloved and a terrier dog fond of farting, and the other a wife, mother of two young sons and an astrophysicist who worked with NASA and who joked with her husband about being painted green, had died. In what can only be described as a twist of fate, they died within hours of each other on the same day.

Startling but not surprising.

You see the women in the group I've been peering in on for months share a bond forged by a common experience I hope never to have. Cancer. Susan had a rare form of breast cancer called inflammatory breast cancer and Rachel died from metastatic breast cancer.

So at today's meeting it wasn't about being unnoticed, it was about removing tentativeness and being seen. It was about applying the lessons of courage I had observed for all those months and showing a measure of respect as well as a demonstration of compassionate solidarity. It was also about giving the spotlight to breast cancer in a way that elevates the plight beyond trite tag lines and pink inspired products. In other words, the people who suffer from cancer as well as their loved ones and even the people who care for them like the doctors, nurses, techs, nutritionists, clergy, scientists and street musicians.

While I too often gripe about my frenzied schedule, the kid's missing homework or the perpetually multiplying wrinkles in my brow, these women are the ones in the real trenches of life. Their membership was decided for them so that now they battle things like brain fog resulting from chemotherapy, the resourceful ways to go to the bathroom when a central line damages the nerves in their arms. They urgently write, when they have enough energy, letters to their children explaining why mommy won't be around for their recitals or weddings but that she loves them more than there are stars in the sky. Sometimes they simply narrate videos when their bodies—not their spirits—have been too ravaged to be able to hold a pen or thought easily. These women plan their funerals trying to choose between BBQ or vegan fare in between preparing and comforting their loved ones. Loved ones, who become the foot soldiers, will have to carry out the tasks when these women are released from membership in the club.

These women are confused. Angry. Philosophic. Fatigued. Happy. Focused. Empathetic. Snarky. Resolved. Hurting. Purposeful. Wise. Grateful. Brilliant.

Above all, they're human.
And humans die.

Life doesn't play fair and she doesn't fight fair either. We all belong to groups but the group I've had membership so far is the one without cancer. There was a recent scare but nothing like receiving a pathology report that reads, "Malignant." Instead of being humbled long enough to focus on that which is truly a priority like living, I get to bitch about things like doors left open so that the power bill equals that of a small country's GDP. It's not that this is inherently bad or their battles inherently noble though their efforts surely are. It's simply about life in all her machinations.

There is good news. Many suffering from this disease do not succumb and actually graduate from this club albeit with physical, emotional and psychic reminders. They hope never to attend a reunion, and they become warriors for new members, supporting them with love, empathy, support and ears.

Today's meeting sobers me. I stare into my computer acutely aware that it's not about me having and them not having. It's about sharing in the experience of grief and gratitude inspired by the stories of Rachel and Susan and the countless others who have since passed, who continue to fight, those who've graduated and for those unwittingly about to join a group that strikes fear in most peoples' hearts.

Six years ago I watched as my mother lay dying in a hospital emergency room from cancer. It's far from pretty. The memories of the short six weeks between diagnosis and death still influence my daily life. Much of it is anguish for her suffering and the lost opportunities. Yet there is great comfort too. What better way to remember to live than to be slugged in the face that you will die sooner than you think.

So today I thank the women in this group. I'll continue to observe from a respectful distance but now I will use whatever opportunities I can to make others aware of the importance of understanding the disease and to seek out the counsel of their trusted healthcare provider regularly. I'm not arrogant enough to think I have any answers whatsoever, but I have been intimately exposed to this disease. I'll never change the world but I will be a positive ripple of awareness to make it better just like these women have done with their strength in suffering.

I'd be dishonest if I said I want to be a part of this group. I don't. However, should I ever be inducted into this membership, I know I will survive no matter the outcome.

Sharon Chayra, Las Vegas
www.chayra.com
Author of *Timeless Beauty* 2013

♥

YOUR APPROACH TO LIFE

Do you wake each morning and throw the bed covers aside with gusto, greeting the sun cheerily, excited at the possibilities the day might offer?

Do you venture out of your house with enthusiasm, chafing at the bit to get started on the day, knowing that around each corner could be something new, something exciting?

At work, do you immerse yourself in your tasks, confident in your abilities? Are you open to helping others, happy to lend a hand, without seeing it as an inconvenience? When challenges crop up, do you give them your full attention, intent on finding the best solutions?

At the end of your work day, do you take a little time for yourself? Do you allow yourself simple little moments when you pause to appreciate some miracle of nature or just behold the beauty of the Earth?

And when you realize you may have found "the one," are you eager to explore what that relationship could offer, open up and allow them into your heart? If you've already found "the one," do you let them know, each and every day, how much they mean to you?

When you find your passion in life, do you pursue it with your entire being, enjoying each step toward your goal, sure in the knowledge that this was what you were meant to achieve?

In short, do you allow yourself to dance through life as though no one is watching?

Jan Hogan, Las Vegas

♥

ONE WAY TO FIT IN

As a male in the spiritual world in Las Vegas, I have always found it hard to find my place at times. The women are strong in the Las Vegas spiritual community. They didn't easily let a strong male in. They left me feeling like an outsider outside. Don't get me wrong I got hugs and gestures of caring. But I found little desire to share feelings, caring or open up. With these feelings, I didn't pursue expanding the relationship beyond this acquaintance. This is not true just of the women in the Las Vegas spiritual arena. I felt the same in other groups where strong males were leading. The feeling of not being accepted was still there in these other areas also.

To feel like I fit in I need to be accepted as I am. I believe this is true for most people. We don't want to change for the people we are meeting to fit in. We want to be accepted.

I realized a lot of these feelings were my choices and my inner voice talking to me. So I made different choices and took responsibility for my feelings. This allowed me to discover that by balancing my male and female energies I was accepted more readily.

This discovery helped me feel like I fit in all the more. With this balanced energy I felt more welcome in these areas.

I discovered by taking responsibility for my choices, I can be happy and fit in anywhere. If I can change and take responsibility for my actions and feelings anyone can.

Take a little responsibility for your choices and have a happy and joyful life.

Jon Carl Olson, Las Vegas
www.jcmpromotions.net

♥

WRITE WITH WONDROUS WORDS WELCOMING WISDOM WILLINGLY!

He looks for Her…Everywhere
He does not see Her…Anywhere
He steps down from the Sky
This Giant
This King
His Footprints all over His World
Impressions left of His search for Her
He asks…Has anyone seen Her
Has anyone found Her
Kept her safe…For Him
His Voice bellows Her Name
Carried by the wind spiraling deep within our minds
Of Her Relationship with Him
Without Her…Who of us is saved,
But He
She was with Him…Always
But not Always with us
Where is Wisdom…Have You found Her?

Vernon J Davis Jr., Las Vegas
www.vernonjdavisjr.com
Author of the *Emosewa Woman* (2nd Edition)

♥

THE TRUTH ABOUT MY MOTHER

I so wanted to help my mother, even while knowing I had no power over her or her addiction to alcohol. At one point, I got the notion that if she would just "see the light" on her own as I had done, she would see she had the ability to heal herself and to begin to have a happy existence. It seemed to me that the therapy she had tried over the last few years had not helped her change.

I decided that I wanted to get her into one of the self-growth weekend workshops I had highly prized in helping me shift my life, so I talked with her for some time, attempting to sway her into attending. She finally acquiesced and signed up for it. I was thrilled. I could see that the end of our suffering was at hand. From my perspective, this was the most potent road and the best I could offer to get her moving in the right direction.

We agreed that she would stay with Sean and me while she attended the workshop. This way, we could more easily support her if she needed it.

Two days before the seminar, we got a call from someone at the organization saying that in going through her
paperwork, they noticed that she was in therapy but had
not included a letter of permission from her psychiatrist
to attend the workshop. As she relayed the story to Sean
and me, she began to cave. Watching her, I could feel my
hopes begin to wane and I started to panic. I said that she
simply must do whatever it would take to get her in the
workshop. We agreed that she would call her psychiatrist
and ask him to write the note. She called and left him
a message; it was the night before the workshop when
he finally called her back. She had her lunch packed and
was ready to go. When he learned what she was intend-
ing to do, he refused to write the letter. He had never experienced the workshop personally but felt she was not
strong enough to be put through this type of thing. She
pleaded with him, but he refused.

Although my mother appeared to be upset by what had
happened, it seemed as if she also felt relieved by not having to attend the workshop. I was utterly devastated. The
next day she packed her things and drove back home.
All my hopes of ever having a functional mother were
gone, and I felt myself let go. Things began to deteriorate
more rapidly for her after this.

One night within a year or so, I got a call from the emergency room. They told me my mother had attempted suicide and that they had just pumped her stomach. This was
her second attempt, and like the first time—while Rick,
her husband, was out of town—she took an overdose of

Valium while drinking vodka, afterward calling the paramedics to rescue her. Her psychiatrist had stopped seeing her, so she was on her own. They told me that she was in their custody for seventy-two hours, and that if I wanted to have her transferred somewhere for help, this would be the time and I would not need her consent. I decided to have her sent to a care unit nearby that dealt with addictions. I knew they would at least dry her out and give her some therapy.

As difficult as it was, the period when my mother was in the care unit was a gift because it was the first time in my life that I witnessed her without alcohol for any length of time. I have vague snippets of memories of her—usually in the morning or early afternoon, before she began to drink—where I can recall her laughing without the encouragement of alcohol, or when she was being lighthearted and playful and singing for me with the quality of voice that let me know she could have been a torch singer.

Over her six-week stay, I got a glimpse into who she really was, mostly by coming to the family counseling nights. In group sessions, the patients and their families would sit in a circle, and one by one the patients would talk about how they were feeling. When she spoke, her voice trembled. She was so quiet that I doubt all could hear her. I heard her, though. For me her voice was a clear as a bell, exposing the enormous amount of pain that was in her heart. Although she was tentative, it appeared that she was at least somewhat willing to be in the process and to look at her life, and from my hopeful perspective, it seemed that perhaps she might embrace this new life. I found her to be funny, quite bright, deeply sensitive, and charming. I really liked this woman. I cherished the time I had with her and looked forward to our future. I began to open up my heart to her again, believing that perhaps her drying out was what she needed. I hoped she would see all that she had missed by being drunk, and that we (her children) were worth working to stay sober for.

Six weeks came and went quickly, and she planned a dinner to celebrate her return. With excitement in my heart, we drove to her house. I couldn't wait to see her sober in her own home and with us children together. I walked inside and could smell something delicious cooking in the kitchen. I made my way to my mother as she bustled away. I said hello, gave her a tight hug, and then it registered: on the counter next to where she was standing was a glass of wine. I gasped as I felt my heart sink. "Mom, I thought you weren't drinking anymore!"

In a lighthearted voice, she said, "Don't worry honey; it's just one glass of wine." I felt a weight hit hard in the room. I had done enough research over the years to know that an alcoholic doesn't just drink one glass of anything, and it wasn't possible that she would stop at a single glass of wine. Still, and probably so that I could make it through the night, I held to the empty hope that it would be just one.

As anticipated, my hope was dashed when within a short

period of time she was back in full swing. Shortly after this, her marriage came to an end. Rick said that he had had enough.

Rick made a good living, and my mother had enjoyed a comfortable lifestyle. Now, however, she would have to downsize and find a place to live on her own. She wanted to live closer to her children, and so she moved into an apartment that was within fifteen minutes from where Sean and I lived. I had concerns about this because I didn't want her drinking to affect our lives more than it already had, but we also felt that having her close would be better if we needed to be of help. So while holding our collective breaths, we helped her move in.

Around that time, I attended a seminar for women only. Throughout the weekend we discussed many of the issues that we, as women, carried through life. I became disturbed in the seminar when one of the women talked about how great her mother was and how her mother was the best thing in her life. I had no such experience, although I wanted it more than I knew how to express. I had had moments of joy with my mother over the years, but they were always cut short when the liquor started to flow. I felt angry and wanted to express the pain I felt around this. I stood up and explained to the group that my mother only cared about herself, and that if she really cared for me, she would stop her drinking for good. I said I wished that she would just learn to cope with her pain so that she could be sober. I could not understand why this was so difficult for her. I sobbed as I heaved out my feelings. Then Diane, the seminar leader, said something that stopped me in my tracks. It was so simple and yet profoundly accurate. She said, "I disagree that your mother hasn't found a way to cope with her pain and suffering." She continued confidently, "Your mother's pain is so deep that talking about it just isn't an option. She obviously doesn't have the tools. Somewhere along the way she discovered that drinking helped her feel better (albeit by numbing). So, in fact, she's dealing with her pain and coping ... the best and only way she knows how."

I remember clearly how her words penetrated me. Within seconds I broke down, unleashing the floodgates, as a powerful wave of compassion came rushing through me. I could see my mother's entire life and how she had lived by coping the best way she knew how. I could feel her profound pain, as well as her desire to have a life that had some semblance of joy in it.

My world and my ongoing experience of her was never the same after that. Although I still had to assert boundaries with her, it now seemed less personal and my resentment toward her waned.

Donna Thomas, Las Vegas
Author of *Pebbles to Pathways: A Journey of Healing the Heart One Insight at a Time*

♥

WINTER ROSES

Early on a cold November Sunday the world waited for me to go and explore. Standing on the porch steps, most of the trees and bushes were nothing more than naked sticks protruding out of the ground. But on the back perimeter of the yard were 7 red roses. They formed the letter "C". My mother's name begins with the letter "C". Years later I realized the roses were meant for me.

I meandered my way through the neighborhood. But it was so cold I went into the Catholic church to get warm. Mass was starting.

A priest in a long white robe stood at the pulpit. He had huge black beads cascading down his robe from his waist. He came from Tanganyika Africa.

Being 10 years old with a vivid imagination and loving Tarzan movies 1 had visions of living in the jungle. I wished I could talk to this man.

To get warm, I headed home to get my gloves. I noticed the red roses. I should cut these and take them to the nuns. I just might get a cookie.

I heard the nuns laughing as I rang the doorbell. No one answered. I rang it again, nothing. I was not getting any warmer and I would not be getting a cookie.

Maybe the priest from Africa will want these. The rectory was close by. I knocked and Ann the cook answered. I gave her the roses to give to the priest. I left for home.

My mother said some priest was calling wanting to speak with me. I had to sit by phone. He called again. He said he had prayed to St. Theresa of the Roses for a sign from God that his work was not in vain. He said I was God's messenger.

He had my address and he would write. Our conversation was short as he had a cab waiting to take him to the airport.

A month later I received a newsletter from him and he related the story about a little girl in the dead of winter bringing him 7 red roses, his answer to a prayer. This newsletter went around the world.

A few years ago I called St. Theresa's parish and spoke to a priest telling him the story. He located a phone number for me so I could speak with Father Tardiff. When he answered I said, "Do you remember a little girl in Pennsylvania that gave you roses in the middle of the winter?" He replied, "I do." I said. "I am that little girl."

We chatted and he had told me he always thought the

roses came from a hothouse. I explained they were the last 7 roses on a bush. He was shocked as it was below zero and yet those roses were very much alive fresh and fragrant.

He later sent me a card in the mail and on it was written: "Memory is the power to gather roses in the winter."

Cynthia Walker, Las Vegas

♥

DEB ASKED WHY

Debra was diagnosed with Cystic Fibrosis (CF) as very young child; she came to realize that she would die at an early age also. At this particular time, Deb, as she liked to be called, was a beautiful young girl but had so many questions about life and yes, death. Many thoughts and questions swirled about in her mind as she wondered why. Why am I sick? Why can't my parents get along? Why do I have to be tossed back and forth between the two people who, I love the very most but, seem to hate each other? Why did they get a divorce, was it because of my disease? Did my bad attitude make them divorce? Is it my fault? Why is my dad getting another divorce from my step-mom that I love? I want to be able to laugh and enjoy life like others do, why can't I seem to be happy like other people are? Why do I have such a bad attitude all the time? Why did I even get this disease? What did I do to deserve this? I know that I didn't do anything to cause my sickness, why was I born this way? Why was I born at all?

My family was gifted with the pleasure and the pain of being a surrogate family for Deb from time to time. She was the younger half-sister of our daughter Brandy (you figure that out). In any case, we had her over for many, many nights, weekends, youth camps and family functions over the years. We really always thought of Deb and treated her as one of our own kids.

Night after night Deb wondered and asked the difficult questions in the hours it took for us to feed her through a tube going into her stomach between her ribs. She had plenty of time to think during several sessions a day when we performed percussions on her back and rib cage. The percussions were to help loosen the accumulation of mucus formed inside the lungs of the victims of CF. It was during these times that we would have in-depth discussions about family, God, life and life's difficult issues.

This horrible disease, in simple terms, slowly hardens the lungs until they flex no more and the victim simply dies of suffocation. Of course, there are several other complications caused by Cystic Fibrosis, such as the inability to fully absorb nutrients, loss of appetite, to name a few. Deb was always under-weight and could never gain weight. The fact that she never felt like eating didn't help at all.

Deb had a wildly smelly stool. Even as a toddler she would literally stink up the whole house. We would always say, "Oh no, Deb's in the bathroom! Clear the house!" It became quite a joke. The smelly poo went on for many years and nobody could figure out why.

One day, her pediatrician sent her to a specialist to do some tests. The late Dr. Reuben Diaz suspected Cystic Fibrosis and his suspicions were confirmed. This was the cause of her digestive problems and her inability to gain any weight and why she was just skin and bones. Suddenly, her stinky stool wasn't so funny after all. It became a daily reminder of the disease that would end her precious life way too early, one day.

We were actively involved in church functions. We worked with the youth group and had lots of fun working with kids for many years on many outings, weekend trips and retreats. Our kids were considered the youth mascots. Deb was able to take advantage of this wonderful environment when she was with us and she absolutely loved the youth group.

I remember one time the youth put on a play at church; it was a Grease themed production. Deb got to play the part of Sandy (Olivia Newton John's part). She was so cute in her little poodle-skirt dancing across the stage in a comedic rendition of this movie that had a spiritual message. Those times were good for Deb, she never had so much fun in her life. Yet when things were quiet she still wondered, why.

Deb's health began to deteriorate, seemingly at a more rapid pace than before. We would administer her percussions more and more often. She coughed and coughed, in an effort to expel this thick mucus that was always growing inside her lungs. She was not able to eat much, so we increased the amount of the food pumped into her stomach through that tube several times a day. She managed to have more fun than ever in youth group but suffered all the more as time went by.

One weekend she went to stay at her dad's house. She was sitting in bed reading the Bible we had given her. She had so many questions swirling around in her head; she just wasn't sure what was real. Was God even real, is this book true? So, she said a prayer that went something like this: "God, if you are real, I need you to prove it to me somehow." She thought for a second and said, "I know, if you are real, turn the light out in my room". Suddenly the light went out. She then said, "Okay, turn it back on" and it came back on. She did this 2 more times, each time it worked. She then wrote in her Bible, "God, tonight you proved yourself to me, I now know that you are real and you love me. Help me to serve you, I love you". When she came back from visiting her dad she told us the story of what had happened and how excited she was to have had this real tangible experience with God. Deb had found a new joy in life because, she knew that she knew. The questions, then, began to fade away.

At age 15 she began to get sicker and sicker. She had to be hospitalized, slipped into a coma and had to be intubated. Dr. Diaz told her parents that they needed to have a family meeting about Deb's condition and ultimate fate, she was dying. Her parents insisted that we were to participate in this meeting as we were after-all her "other" parents. We had to make the decision to remove Deb from life support that day. We said our good-byes, wept and told her we knew she would be waiting for us in Heaven.

In preparation for her funeral, Pastor David asked us for her Bible. As Pastor David was speaking of memories of Deb, he said, "I was looking through Deb's Bible and I found what she wrote last year, it reads, "God, tonight you proved yourself to me, I now know that you are real and you love me. Help me to serve you, I love you." Just as he finished that quote, a clap of thunder came from outside and the lights went out, yes, 3 times (just like in her bedroom). Nobody else, but we, knew the back-story behind what Deb had written in her Bible that lonely night some months before. In fact, we had kind of forgotten about it until this all happened and reminded us of that night.

We began telling her parents, the rest of the family and friends what had happened and the story behind why she had written those words in her Bible. Each of them would gasp and begin to cry as they realized and understood what had just happened. We also told Pastor David.

He said he was drawn to read that statement and felt it was special. Hmmm...

Skeptical? Sure, the lights go out often during thunder storms, right? The thing is it was a perfectly sunny day, no clouds when we walked into the funeral home that afternoon. Further, when we walked out one hour later it was also bright and sunny, not a cloud in the sky. However, only the parking lot was soaking wet, nothing else in sight was wet from the rain, or should I say, Reign?

Dan Klatt, Las Vegas
www.DanRKlatt.com
Author of *A Painless Detox, No More Excuses*

♥

EGO AND EMOTION, HEALING AND ENLIGHTENMENT

This work in progress is the result of over 35 years study of ancient and modern texts on psychology, religion, spirituality and self-help, as well as the close observation of the ego and spiritual process from within. The author has always instinctively sought the most powerful keys to unlocking the chains of the ego mind, understanding the secret nature of emotion, the role of thinking and the role of not thinking in healing the emotions and even enlightenment.

Surveying everything from ancient Tibetan Buddhist texts to modern day self-help therapy, the book reveals the key patterns and essential methods that both keep the false ego in place and which can be used to unlock the mind, heart and spirit as a powerful synergy, each playing their "proper roles" in one's life in this world as we move toward realizing our ultimate freedom and power to live as we prefer.

The book looks at Tibetan and Indian sutras, the Bible, Christian contemplative writings, A Course in Miracles,

Krishnamurti, nearly-lost (add hyphen between these 2 words) Jewish teachings, meditation, Sufi teachings, Zen, Taoism, Egyptian mysteries, Tolle and other modern authors, revealing an illuminating and affirming commonality that empowers one with a certainty of what works and what doesn't on the path of awakening.

What is the true nature of the ego? What is negative emotion and how do we leave it behind? What is the cause of and "cure" for the illusion of separation? What is the ideal role of the mind in the path to awakening? What are the essential "methods" of awakening? What is the one principle that runs through all the great and effective teachings of all ages and spiritual paths? This book aims to reveal the universal pattern of consciousness in a very convincing and usable way.

Author: Eric J Tischler has devoted his life to understanding life and what it takes to make it "better" both inwardly and outwardly. He started his studies of spirituality and psychology at the age of 15, and has had a talent for recognizing key patterns, themes and elements in both writings and experiences. Highly intuitive, he also has a mind and life that is very balanced between left and right brain natures. He plays Scottish snare drum in a bagpipe and drum band, plays alto recorder, paints, practices Taiji, is studying French, is pretty dandy with a computer, and thinks and observes a lot.

Eric J Tischler, Las Vegas
www.livinginfocus.net

♥

MAKING VEGAS HOME

I arrived in Las Vegas almost 3 years ago now. At the time I was a military wife (British married to an American Airman). We have a beautiful daughter together - Gracie, who is now 5 years old. Gracie was born with ventriculomegaly, a condition of the brain that was diagnosed during my pregnancy. She was given 70 percent chance of severe to moderate disability and at one point was even told she may not survive full term. This news devastated us. That, coupled with the long periods of absence and eventually the big move of immigrating to the United States, gradually resulted in the eventual disintegration of our marriage. This happens to many couples that are married in the military. The problem was that this happened around five months after moving to Las Vegas.

I realized I was alone and fighting a nasty custody battle. I was desperate to return home. This was the agreement by my daughter's father before leaving the UK. However, he changed his mind, and I was no longer allowed to leave the country. I barely slept for weeks and cried most of the time. I was probably in shock because I don't remember much else during this period in my life. I felt very alone and scared I would not see my daughter for a long time.

I was not allowed to leave the country with her and since I could not drive, had no job and was still waiting for the legal documents to enable me to do so, I was stuck.

Through the kindness of strangers, many of whom are now friends, a good lawyer and a wise judge I was awarded custody and a small amount of alimony for 9 months. This gave me a timeline to pass my driver's test, save for a car and find a job. I did not manage all of this in 9 months so we stayed with an old friend of mine.

I was able to find a job working on the strip as a black-jack dealer. But I was on call a lot and wasn't making the money I needed to rent our own home. However, I had an apartment up for sale in the UK and after being on the market for a year, it sold! As quickly as I could I went condo-hunting with the small amount of equity I pulled out of it and managed to find a condo for sale for the exact same amount of money I had made from the sale. I fought for that little condo and with a lot of determination and hope I found myself with the keys a few weeks later. We had gone from having nowhere to live to owning our own place outright. And as time went on, I got better at my job and found myself with more hours. And, as luck would have it we were zoned for one of the best public elementary schools in Clark County too.

So, here we are, me and my daughter, 3 years later. In our own home, I managed to get a car with NO credit on good faith. And I managed to pay that off too. I'm still working on building credit and getting financially stable but I have my little girl and she is thriving. She has a ton of friends and so do I. Las Vegas embraced me with open arms when I had nothing and knew no one. It picked me up during a time I had lost everything. Call it luck, God, or just sheer determination, call it what you want. I adapted and changed to survive the situation I was in. And the best news is my daughter is doing better than I ever could have hoped for. Gracie, by the way, has no disabilities. She is in fact two grades ahead in school for her age and is excelling academically at a vast rate. I am so proud of her. As so is everyone who knows and loves her. Not being able to return to the UK was the best thing that could have happened to us. I thank her father for two things: my beautiful daughter and forcing me to develop the strength and courage to overcome my ordeal on my own.

Anette Lachowski, Las Vegas
www.anettelachowski.com

♥

BACK FROM BROKEN

"You can have it all, my empire of dirt."

We all suffer from pain, physical and emotional; we have all been hurt; it is the price we pay for having a beating heart. It takes constant effort for me to allow the beauty of life not to be overshadowed by the pain. I live my life reveling in the glory that I have faced my deepest fears and survived the wounds of my past.

I have understanding now, at age forty-two, that my "ideal childhood" was riddled with horror. I never understood unconditional love because my role from infancy had become the pleaser. From the days that I sucked on my pacifier, I became just that, a "miracle child" brought into this world to quell all the pain of my mother's past. She depended on me for her joy. I carried the burden of keeping the queen happy so that the kingdom may live at peace. Raised in a household that lifted you up, only to knock you down, was my previous definition of what it means to be loved. The hollowness and confusion of psychological abuse is perhaps the bitterest pill to swallow. Time and knowledge have helped me digest my truth, but not living in a state of anger is my greatest challenge.

Terror is palpable fear and horror, on the other hand it inspires feelings of dread and confusion as it lurks. The uncertainty disturbs the mind and allows anger to seep in. It lived in me for forty years, until it nearly destroyed me. My anger incubated in my spine until I hit rock bottom. The cascade of my vertebrae caused me to research the origin of my anger. Held up by two metal rods and sixteen screws, I now have the ability to stand tall against abuse. It was a challenge for me to realize the purity of determination, as opposed to anger that had driven me to succeed in life because I knew nothing else. Maturity, time, love and awareness have helped me to understand that the years I lived drunk and stoned in a cloud of anger were not "my fault". Coping with pain is every individual's battle in this life.

At age two my poker face was learned as a means of disguising my pain and anger. I became a master, a chameleon with the ability to fit in everywhere because I deprived myself of my authenticity. Somewhere along the road of life, my needs and wants were overrun by my incessant need to please others. On my journey into this bright future, I find great comfort in knowing that life can be happy and there is beauty all around us if you choose to see it. It is your choice. Abuse enables the brain to create a "survival mode" as a means of protection. It kicks into auto-pilot and those that are abused are not even aware of it. As a person that was blessed enough to come back from broken, I have learned that people that are broken, do often not even know that they are broken.

Survival mode is propelled by the ego, thus humility and its entire splendor, is obliterated. I write to convince myself that I am no longer broken and to inspire others to see the light. I had mastered hiding my pain behind a beautiful smile and at the end of the day, I had no energy left to enjoy the graces life had provided for me. In this lifetime, I am proud to say that good has triumphed over evil. Positivity, purity and love have prevailed over my demons, that being said, I will relay my message: my goodness and strength overpowered the weak and the damaged. Be mindful that the waitress that serves you dinner, or the gentleman sitting beside you on the bus, or the customer you serve in your retail job, may be grasping at straws to hold onto life. Be kind to strangers/friends/loved ones, watch your words and your temper, try to fill your days with goodness and you will be rewarded.

Lila Penn, Las Vegas

♥

TO RUSSIA WITH LOVE

"I've met the most wonderful woman and we are getting married. Can you come to our wedding?" It was a simple invitation to the wedding of my friend Dan, who is an American and his beloved Jean, who is Russian and lives in Russia.

Russia? Isn't that the place all the bad guys in American action films are from?

At the time of invitation Russia was not even on my "desired travel destination" list. I have learned over the years that God does not present such an opportunity to be taken lightly. So I prayed about it.

As they planned the details of their wedding, I was being told by concerned friends many negatives about traveling to Russia along with horror stories. They painted a picture implying as an American I would receive a poor reception in Russia.

I've traveled all over the world with no fear yet the language barrier and the inability to read the signs presented itself as a challenge in my mind. I was told not many people speak English and I did not speak Russian. I accepted the challenge pushing aside the unproductive thoughts.

I continued to pray. I am a very optimistic person with a great love for people and an adventurous nature. My intention was to travel from Las Vegas to Russia with love in my heart believing that I would be well received.

Russia became an adventure! As I researched sights of interest and began selecting hotels and modes of transportation I knew this was a God-planned adventure. My preparation steps went very smoothly including my visa application.

With my passport, visa and boarding pass in hand I headed to McCarran Airport for a nearly 24 hour journey to Krasnodar, Russia. Two plane changes stood between me and my first trip to "Mother Russia" as it's often referred.

I accented my journey with a smile. This is how I greeted my seat-mates, other travelers in line, the airport and airline employees, with a smile. It's difficult to convey love without a smile on your face and in your heart.

My cheeks were getting a workout from smiling as I arrived at the Krasnodar airport. I walked down the stairs from the plane on to the Tarmac and inhaled the fresh humid air. The surrounding greenery was breathtaking.

Four smiling faces greeted me as I exited the baggage

claim. Kate, John, Earl and his wife Dana came up to me and gave me a hug saying "Welcome to Russia". They were friends of Dan and Jean. Thankfully Earl and Kate spoke English very well.

We traveled by car while getting acquainted as we looked at miles and miles of open green fields with livestock, corn, and sunflowers coloring the landscape. When our vehicle pulled into the driveway of Jean's house all of her roommates and friends came out to greet me.

Over the days leading up to the wedding I engaged in deeply bonding conversation with my new Russian friends. We had family style meals and I learned about the customs and culture of Russia. The wedding celebration was beautiful. A first-hand account of true Russian living can never be replaced by a television travel show. I felt so welcomed and very happy I followed my heart and went.

When given the chance to have a daring adventure, choose adventure.

Tamia Dow, Las Vegas
Chaplain for the International Association of Women Police
www.iawp.org

♥

CHOICES AND CHANGES

I love women. I love how we are up, down, sideways, joyful and sad all within a matter of minutes sometimes. What I love most about women is how much we cherish and adore our best friends. We make a great best friend. When a bestie calls to say "I need…" our answer is "yes" before we even let them finish their sentence. We treat our best friends like they are deserving of the best of everything because we know they truly are. Whatever they need, we are there for them. We love them with all our hearts and believe in them with every fiber of our being. We would move mountains for them if that is what would ease their burden. We love them unconditionally and accept them for being the vulnerable, mistake-making perfectly imperfect women that they are.

Why is it that we have such a challenging time treating ourselves with that same unconditional love and support? For some reason, we don't believe that we are worth that same level of care and kindness. We are generally not gracious receivers, and we so easily find fault with ourselves.

Guess what? We can choose to see ourselves differently.

We can choose to just let the negative self-talk go. Guess what else? We are amazing just the way we are! Are we perfectly imperfect? Yes! How do we become believers that we are already magnificent? We just choose to believe it. We make choices each and every day...actually we make hundreds of choices every day. Isn't it time to start choosing to see how amazing you are rather than choosing to see where you are lacking?

Did God mess up and create imperfect human beings to inhabit this earth? No. Are we perfect people doing imperfect things and thinking imperfect thoughts? Yes. That doesn't make us imperfect, so how about if we choose to define ourselves as perfectly imperfect instead? Choosing a different belief about your own amazingness is completely up to you! How fabulous would it be if when you looked into a mirror, you saw your best friend looking back at you?

I believe that it's okay to be selfish. We learned at an early age that being selfish wasn't such a good thing. Well, I think that being selfish is a great thing! There is a difference between being selfish and being self-absorbed. Self-absorbed – not such a good thing. Taking care of you FIRST is really important. It's exactly like the flight attendants tell us when we are just about to lift off...put your own oxygen mask on first!

How amazing will it be to live in a world surrounded by peaceful, self-loving, and enlightened women? Picture our smiles forever radiant, our eyes bright and wide, and our collective enthusiasm intoxicating as we share who we truly are with each and all. This is how we change the world one person at a time.

Janet Dunnagan
www.journeytobutterfly.com
Author of *You Get It When You Get It...My journey from caterpillar to butterfly* and the companion *My Caterpillar to Butterfly Journal*

♥

A MOTHER'S JOURNEY

For the birth of our first child, my partner David and I had planned a calm, natural water birth at a local hospital. Ten hours into labor, as I was waiting for my doula, Naomi, to arrive and set up our birthing tub, a hospital nurse came into the room to check my progress. She discovered that my son was in breech position, and informed me that I was going to have an emergency caesarean.

I asked the nurse if I could have a moment to think, and she retorted, "What do you need to think about?" Trying to stick to my birth-plan, I asked her if I could get up and move around, so I could try and get the baby to flip naturally--She barked, "This is life or death! There are no options." What the nurse said filled me with fear, and every fiber in my being screamed, "Run!"

My doula, Naomi finally arrived, after telling her what the hospital nurse had said I asked her if I had any options. Without success, Naomi attempted to locate a doctor willing to allow me to deliver my baby vaginally and naturally. Naomi then called a midwife with home-birth breech experience. David and I informed the hospital staff that we would be leaving, and headed home to deliver our son.

Within forty-five minutes of being home, my labor was becoming more intense, with contractions coming harder and faster. I was happy to be home, but still concerned about my child's delivery. Was I really as strong as I thought? Was my body going to know how to birth a breech baby? As these thoughts rushed through my head, I felt a hand touch my shoulder, and a wave of calmness and a sense of light poured through my body. I turned and saw a beautiful woman, "Hello, I am Marve, and I will be your midwife. How are you doing?" I instantly felt more relaxed, and regained my sense of empowerment. Marve reminded me to trust in myself and in my body as I continued to labor. An hour and a half later, my first child Lochlan was born.

Through Naomi O'Callaghan and Marvelys Lopez, I was introduced to an entire community of women in Las Vegas. I have hope for the future knowing these women, and knowing they are making informed choices. We may not all agree on everything, or have had the same birth experiences but we do agree that the way a woman births her children should be her choice.

Through informing myself about my birth options, I learned there are many differing opinions about birth. Knowing your options allows you to have power during the extremely vulnerable experience of childbirth. As a result of my own experiences, I am inspired daily to keep paying forward through my at-home business, Know Mommy. My mission is to help women learn about their birth/parenting options so the choice they make will be theirs.

Janelle Ross, Las Vegas
www.knowmommy.blogspot.com

♥

ENTERING THE GOLDEN AGE OF JOY, TRANSFORMING THE DARK AGE OF CONDEMNATION

Do you see that sun rising on the horizon? Do you feel warm rays touching you begging to light up your day? Can you hear the harmonic sounds of nature as the breeze flows through the grasses tickling your legs and feet? Is there a sense of joyful well-being that titillates every cell in your body?

Expect Joy and Joy Will Find You!

We are the healers, teachers, mentors, up lifters, visionaries and innovators who have entered a new age with vision, certainty, and desire. This new age is a Golden Age that will rival anything we have ever known before. We are the carriers of the Radiant Heart. The Legacy Of Light pioneered by The Compassionate Heart of Buddha, the Christ Consciousness, The Enlightened Heart of Yogananda, The Determined Heart of Moses, The Song Of Rumi, The Heart of the Great Spirit our Grandmothers and Grandfathers, The Eternal Heart of the Source of All

That Is. Expect Love and Love wills Flow through You and From You!

Alignment with the fundamental consciousness of Joy is our work in the coming years. Joy is the flame of life that caused us to want to be born into this beautiful world. It is the fire that burns within us to reach for a better way, a more fulfilling way to live. Igniting this flame is our life's purpose, to live from the Radiant Heart of All That Is, IS OUR JOY!

"When you find vibrational alignment with you, you personally thrive. You feel good; you look good; you have stamina; you have energy; you have balance; you have clarity; you have wit; you have abundance of all things that you consider to be good. You thrive in all ways when you come Into Energy Balance with the True You. Vibrational Relativity - that's what it's all about."
—*Abraham*

Deliberately Aligning With Joy. This is our work, to deliberately align with Joy by making it a priority in our daily life until it is second nature to us. In my life I seek expansion in everything I do, expanding from unhappiness in myself, my world and my body. I can honestly say that over the three decades I have consciously sought after the elusive Joy Factor, I have finally come to realize its value in my life and in the heart of humanity. I am a teacher, a visionary and an open channel for higher wisdom. While writing my recent book on Activate Joy, Live Your Life Beyond Limitations I had to stretch further than I have ever stretched in my life. In Meditation one morning I simply asked this question. "How do you do it? How do you stay in the Christ Consciousness of unconditional love?" This swift answer caused an expansion within me that is at the basis of this writing. I heard, "Bless everything and condemn nothing."

Our society, our world consciousness has its value system based in a negative self-esteem belief system. *"I will devalue myself and others so I can feel better about myself."* There is not much joy in that, which is why people struggle to find happiness. Condemnation of others and ourselves seems second nature, the natural place to go. This is what I am calling our Dark Age, righteous indignation, condemning the actions of others to the point of the destruction of the creative spirit on all levels. Just look at our news and contemplate our condemning consciousness. To expand into Joy, self-reflection is imperative. Condemnation must recede into irrelevance.

One of the areas of interest to me is Mastery. We are not born into this world a Master. That requires practice, dedication and a willingness to constantly reflect on our thoughts and our heart space as we A.I.M., for higher thoughts and inspiration.

"The path to happiness and a sense of well-being in this very life lies not in avoiding suffering but in using the conscious, embodied, direct experience of it as a vehicle to gain deep insight into the true nature of life and your own existence." Realizations of Buddha

A door was opened for me a few years ago, a thought that would turn my life around and allow me to be able to bring this teaching to the world in just this way. Oftentimes ideas and inspirations come to us and we slough them off. As you learn the Art of Mastery you will honor every thought and idea that is offered as you do the air you breathe, as life itself. I have developed a relationship with my Deep Intuitive Self and I pay close attention to the direction in which I am pointed, and I offer this to you as well...

Embrace Differences with Enthusiasm. I remember the first time I brought this idea into a Mastery class I was teaching. It stunned my group. The wall we hit is this, "I can't condone the actions of... because..." We are so programmed with others' ideas of morality that to condemn seems natural, it is accepted and even expected behavior. Energetically here is what happens when we venture down the road of condemnation:

The heart closes. The Radiant Fire of Unconditional Love is dimmed to almost nothing. Rage rules. There is no True Joy! Instead there is the false and fake joy of revenge that leaves us empty with nowhere to go.

There is a basic tenet (rule) that has been missed in the collective, until now. No one can be born for you and no one can die for you. There is YOU. You cannot control anything outside of yourself and you have no <u>real</u> power over anything, except you and your feelings about what is happening in your world.

The Golden Age of Joy Embraces Life on All Levels. Mastery is calling us. Mastery is showing each creative soul that their expression is inviolate, unique and blessed. Mastery offers a radical inner shift in how you view your existence. My passion is to consistently bring awareness to JOY as an attainable consciousness for my world and myself. Practicing embracing differences with enthusiasm has given me the freedom within my own heart to allow others to express themselves... freely. I am not telling you that you won't be challenged because you will. So I will give you three foundational tenants from my Radiant Heart to bring you out of the Dark Age of condemnation and into the Golden Age of Joy.

One – Always look for the gift in any situation. This will cause your heart to open and your eyes to look up. Acknowledge that this may be hard for you in the moment, so ask within... "Teach me to see the light in this situation." Whatever I think is real is irrelevant to my higher awareness of Joy. Now in the stillness... allow the glimmer of light to stream in. Sometimes it will be a word, an image or a thought. Follow it; allow it to lead you...

Two– Pay attention to your own triggers because that will show you where there is uplifting that needs to be done within you. What we see in the world is a reflection of our innermost thoughts and beliefs. Mastery allows relief from fear-based thoughts by bringing attention to the blessings in life.

Three– Tell a New Story! As you review the unwanted

energy showing itself to you, tell a new story with hope and a story that completely says what you really want as an experience in your life. Short and Sweet does it.

Example: A woman is constantly telling a story of her father and his female companion, complaining that the woman taking care of her father is controlling him and his money. On the other hand she profusely acknowledges how much the woman does for her elderly father relieving her of that immediate pressure. When we are on the cycle of condemning anything or anyone, the result is confusion and the pain is no resolution, not being able to align with either side or the cycle continues.

Condemning anything becomes addictive because it feeds into the negative self-esteem consciousness of devaluing others to make you feel better.

The woman's new story: "I have a wonderful relationship with my father, and I am glad I don't have to take care of him."

Joy Equals Freedom! Freedom Allows Joy!
Realize this, you are a world unto yourself and so is everyone else. Master the ART of Celebration and Dance. Make your Joy-World a priority.
The Golden Age of Joy is Here, Embrace It!

Dr. AlixSandra Parness, DD
www.activatejoy.com
Author of *Active Live Your Life beyond Limitations*

♥

FREEDOM

Freedom, a word used by many individuals for many purposes; a word riddled with meanings; overtones, undertones...

Live free or die! Freedom isn't free. I'd rather die on my feet than live on my knees. Choice or the freedom to choose? When navigating to a point in space or time there are many millions of points of course correction; these cannot fairly be considered choices as the choice was to begin and where to go, course corrections are the journey. In the navigation of life there are many millions of choices. For many billions of our brothers and sisters daily choices are finding safe shelter, a safe bit of water to drink or for food preparation if there is food. How can a human be free to think and choose if the most basic needs of food, water, shelter and the safety of self and family are not secure?

The human species is tribal. One need not be a social scientist to see the tribal nature of mankind. It is a protection mechanism woven into the fabric of society so deeply that it could be considered as fundamental as our genetic code. It is integrated into our subconscious as to be fundamental to consciousness. Those people coming down the trail do not look like, sound like, dress like, believe like my tribe therefore they are a possible threat; beware of strangers. This tribal instinct paralyzes choice; subverts personal freedom; crushes critical thinking.

Under the principle of law, "All men are created equal." A great republic was founded in the 18th century exulting this principle of law which might neutralize the tribal nature to enhance personal freedom. The republic would bring about a social basis where people are free to believe and live as they choose within a system of law to which all are equally responsible. The tribal effect controls the consciousness it paralyzes government. How does one find personal freedom in such a state of affairs? When our religion, race, family, community, club/gang, social structure, sexuality, economy are different from "those people".

Anyone reading this most likely does not have dyer choices to be made each day relative to clean water, personal safety and food. Making the choice of how you live is yours. Are we controlled by tradition, myth, pier groups, that are how it has always been. My daddy taught me, if it was good enough for him, it is good enough for me. Trapped in a deeply interwoven structure of consciousness unable to do anything but follow? It is painful to step out of this structure. It is scary. To be an outcast in the pre-historic tribal world was a death sentence and the human consciousness knows this, conform, follow or die. The good news is you can choose. You can think; choose your path; choose your thoughts. A fine man said, "A leader is first a leader of self". It takes courage, and you have all you need to proceed.

Anonymous
Submitted by John Tyler, Las Vegas

♥

WHEN DO YOU KNOW LIFE AS YOU INTEND IT TO BE?

When you decide to understand you have choices, you take a new path. As we are souls living a human experience, we have the power of God, Spirit, Source, Infinite Intelligence, the higher power that is greater than any man. The Universe, Mother Nature, and the source we are organically connected to. Yet we abuse it, ignore it, and even discard the power.

Mankind created this enemy, and then turned the enemy on themselves, only to create self-destructing or self-defeating thoughts, habits, and behaviors. Meaning, we lead ourselves away from the most important attribute we have to survive the dissonance, which is our truth, the true purpose of our existence here on earth.

We have been taught to fight, have wars, to judge, to hate, to resent, hold remorse and become bitter. This is the EGO, the dark side, and the shadow that resides in each and every one of us that has taken over the majority of society. Yet we also have the light, love, brightness, and truth side as well, and it is up to all of US, meaning Humanity to change it.

We have choices to follow our heart which is our soul's purpose. Joyful is our natural state of being as the human species on this planet, yet we have been subjected to conformity, confinement, suppression, isolation and judgment. We have been plugged into this massive downward spiral to become the walking dead. People's spirit has been chastised and castrated due to false beliefs and they don't even know it.

When you understand this, it is Time to Wake Up! Wake up to the life you want. Be willing to be part of the change. Give Peace and Love a chance, and it starts with you. See life with new eyes. Hear words of a different language. Speak in a way that will spread Love and kindness. Touch in a way that you have never touched before. Really feel your true emotions of pure unconditional love and share it with others. Taste the wonderment of the food you eat and drink, and appreciate the nutritional value it gives you. And, lastly just be be in the moment. Be with the one's you love, be one with God and the Universe, and be one with each other as we are all created equal interconnected to each other.

We have all been blessed with a GOD given Talent, a talent that needs to be used to create prosperity and abundance for all. Find it and USE it. Remember, One Nation under GOD, the Universe, our Source, and our Infinite Intelligence we have all been blessed with. The time is

NOW, to eliminate the imbalance, find LOVE, share LOVE, and Be LOVE, Be Intentional with everything's you think, say and do, and just imagine what we can do as a collective consciousness, yes, change the world!!!! So are you in?
Namaste'

Mary Chambers, Las Vegas

♥

TREASURES OF WONDER INSPIRATIONS FROM LAS VEGAS

Life within this mystical oasis has given me many blessings. One must look beyond the obvious to see the true beauty that fabricates our existence. Once you have surrendered to the voice of nature, magically the lights dim and the skies begin to glow with all the illuminating stars of the universe. In the distance you can hear the howling cry of a coyote gathering her cubs, and in the brush, soft coos of rustling quail nesting for the night.

As I stand tall, overlooking our vibrant city, I reflect on all that makes life wonderful. This brings me peace.

I have always gravitated to the evening's sky, and the moonlit nights of this fair valley. There is something very sacred in the setting of the sun on the horizons of such purple beauty, always with Mother Nature's offering of a magnificent painting at the end of each day, given freely to all of us only to be enjoyed as it fades to black.

While bathing in the moonlight, I reflect on the hurried-
ness of the day, all the while wondering, "If only everyone
could take a moment and look beyond the façade that
claims so many souls, perhaps they too could rest peacefully."

I have found a well of stillness within the valley that never sleeps, a place where one can be so close to the light
that attracts the moth, yet so far away that the whispers
of the ancient mountain echoes in your soul.

Yes, this is an amazing oasis, and beyond the chaos of
the neon glow rests the treasures of wonder and beauty,
God's greatest gifts…

Jacie Urquidi-Maynard, Las Vegas

♥

ODE TO KENNY

One month ago today
Your sweet soul passed away
Silently in the night
Your spirit took flight
Then soared into light
With Mama you reunite
And returned to
Father's arms
Free from pain, free from harm
Before you passed
Your love did cast
Perpetual memory
Of whom you chose to be
A good person and man
Letting me hold your hand
In your final moment
Was heavenly,
God-sent

Rest in Peace Big Sexy aka Kenny
My brother
My protector

Glen Alex, Las Vegas
08.05.13

NOTE FROM THE AUTHOR

As I was laying out the final pages for this book, I received this submission from Glen Alex and thought it was the perfect way to close the book. It reminded me that life is short and you never know how long you have on this earth. Each day remember to recognize the loved ones in your life that inspire, motivate, challenge and encourage you along your life journey with celebration and love!

Love & Light,

Lori Chaffin

Lori Chaffin

This page is intentionally left blank for you, the reader. What is your wish for humanity? Thank you for reading our loving words, and for recording your own.

_____

_____

_____

_____

_____

_____

_____

_____

_____

_____

_____

_____

_____

_____

_____

_____

_____

_____

259

www.ingramcontent.com/pod-product-compliance
Lightning Source LLC
Chambersburg PA
CBHW060044100426
42742CB00014B/2692